THE ULTIMATE BOOK OF GUNFIGHTING

A PRACTICAL GUIDE TO DEFENDING YOURSELF

ROBERT K. CAMPBELL

Skyhorse Publishing

Skyhorse Publishing books may be purchased in bulk at special discounts for sales promotion, corporate gifts, fund-raising, or educational purposes. Special editions can also be created to specifications. For details, contact the Special Sales Department, Skyhorse Publishing, 307 West 36th Street, 11th Floor, New York, NY 10018 or info@skyhorsepublishing.com.

Skyhorse® and Skyhorse Publishing® are registered trademarks of Skyhorse Publishing, Inc.®, a Delaware corporation.

Visit our website at www.skyhorsepublishing.com.

10 9 8 7 6 5 4 3 2 1

Library of Congress Cataloging-in-Publication Data is available on file.

Cover design by Tom Lau
Cover photo credit Robert K. Campbell

Print ISBN: 978-1-5107-0319-3
Ebook ISBN: 978-1-5107-0320-9

Printed in China

CONTENTS

DEDICATION

This book is the result of many years of experience. No one knows better than I that the names of trainers and authors are symbols for many men who have worked together to perfect a craft. On a personal level, there isn't any possibility I would have had the inspiration and ability to do this type of work without the support of my family. To my wonderful Joyce, always by my side and in my thoughts. She stood by me as I compressed a lifetime of experience into a few chapters. My children are diverse in personality but always an inspiration to be all I can be. My granddaughter Chinoya spent much of her day with me as I wrote this book; thanks for her sweet attitude and good company.

You might say the book is over forty years in the making. Thanks to my grandparents who were generous with a mature and trustworthy young man; the late Wilburn Williams gave me firearms experience, and Maude Williams took me to safe shooting areas. My mother, Mary Ellen Campbell, took me to the library, book stores, and gun stores. My father, the late Robert Campbell Sr., made certain I obtained a good education, without which I would not have been able to pursue a writing or professional career.

My grandmother was the most peaceful and faithful woman I have ever known.

> When a strong man, fully armed, guards his own palace, his goods are safe.
>
> —Luke 11:21

She prayed a mantle over me and my sons, and it has preserved us. From New York to Korea, Kosovo, and points in between, and facing shots in the dark, we have remained safe. Common-sense training has served us. This book is humbly dedicated to the family I love so well.

—Robert Campbell

INTRODUCTION

Those of you who have purchased this book have done so, I hope, with a desire to learn effective skills for personal defense. Personal defense and combat shooting as disciplines are important skills and have little in common with target shooting. Target shooting is a waltz; combat shooting is karate. I hope this book will be of service to armed professionals, as well as busy people looking for good information. I never lose sight of the fact that I am training people for survival.

You should train hard, but short, systematic practice sessions will work well. The trial-and-error method of practice is a long and costly means of learning. There is a positive correlation between prior training and survival in a gunfight. Training must be demonstrably well balanced. I wish to orient the reader toward reality. Training must be rational in spirit. Speculation on tenable presumptions is part of the game, but the real world always must be our first consideration. When you challenge the dead eyes of a killer, you had best have skills in place.

Training has been an ongoing, continuous education for the author. Training should have a dual aim: both skill building and personal development as an individual. I think that a book is only good with an original and personal vision, and I am certain you will find that in these pages. While there is room for personal adaptation of drills, there should be no doubt and no dispute that these skills are well suited to personal defense. This means dynamic training rather than static training. As you read this book, challenge any preconceived notions you have of technique. Take every tactic to the range. An hour of range work is worth weeks of discussion. Never lose sight of the best solution: The best outcome in any confrontation is that no shots are fired, and there is no loss of life.

This book teaches the necessary skills needed in a worst-case scenario. Many of our adversaries among the criminal element have such an intimacy with violence that there is no chance of untangling this dependence. They may suffer from general illiteracy, but they are street erudite. They are a deadly threat. This book is not without dark pages to describe these sociopaths. Citizens who are too passive to organize a defense against such felons will be helpless. The goal is to organize and put together a repertoire of necessary skills. We use reason and logic to determine which skills are needed. Conversely, we face an adversary without normal ideas of motivation and devoid of a moral compass. They do not understand the moral impact of their actions.

When discussing personal defense, there is an inexhaustible mine of theoretical topics offered by amateurs. Some have one-sided knowledge. You cannot learn such important skills from individuals who lack first-hand, practical experience. Avoid a heavy investment in those who have only attended training schools. Seek out those who have witnessed violence and participated in critical battles. Schools and training are essential. I also wish to learn from those who become experts through survival. When the object of your fear becomes the subject or your fear, it is too late to learn skills. Yet many have found themselves in just such a situation without an idea of how to act.

Much of what I have read in the popular press invites skepticism among professionals. Keep an open mind and honest skepticism, but also use the logic ladder. Does this make sense? Compare the logic ladder to unrealistic threat assessment, and you will understand the need for realistic training. I have not addressed my training toward theoretical concepts but to answer what actually happens during a lethal assault. To become proficient at arms requires a commitment on a higher plane than a video game. Don't ask if weapon craft is a science or an art. A science is primarily analytical, while an art is synthetic. Perhaps we have a little of both in weapon craft. Abstractions of science must always be alloyed with an understanding of human nature.

When learning different drills, and developing skill through muscle memory and repetition and reapplication of these drills, hard work and diligent training isn't free of mental tension. During a critical incident, you seldom retain full comprehension. The tyranny of the moment, as it is called, takes its toll. Determination and concentration are required in practice. The single, greatest determiner of survival during a critical incident is prior training. Gunfights create odd disarrangements of perspective. Diligent practice and complete familiarity with the handgun allow you to retain a relationship of normal proportion and properties with your best performance. When you are fighting, you are fighting two people: yourself and the adversary. An armed felon has already made the decision to kill. Your training will prepare you to save your life. Your determination to survive will allow you to implement these skills. There is endless interest in personal defense, but there are doers and there are readers. Be a reader *and* a doer. In this book are skills that are relevant to saving your life, with an emphasis on relevance for everyday life. When looking for authoritative guidance, beware of underdeveloped ideas.

There are three primary concerns other than marksmanship, and these lead to proficiency with the handgun. These are safety, speed, and concealment. A misstep in safety procedure may be as deadly as a felon's bullet. Concealment is a requirement of daily carry. Speed may be vital to the timely application of skills. In these pages you will learn how to develop these skills.

You will also find many recommendations for equipment. I endorse only service-grade equipment. When you have a reliable handgun, shooting development takes a more direct pathway. The gear must be proven in service. I also recommend only powerful and effective handguns. You should not be under-gunned. Felons have shown an ability to absorb punishment that seems at odds with physiology. In simple terms, bad guys sometimes need a lot of shooting. The skills you learn are important and will impact your survival in a positive manner. A good handgun, a proper holster, and effective ammunition are all important. The man or woman behind the gun is the vital element.

Despite the grim nature of the task confronted by those who must defend their person or their family against felons, a fact remains: life is precious. This book focuses on the tactics to save your life rather than the legal ramifications of the act. Just the same, before you carry a handgun, there are self-examinations to endure. The moral imperative demands that you will fire only when there is no other choice. The need to stop the adversary's actions must be so great that it cannot matter, morally or legally, if that attacker dies as a result of being stopped.

In our society there are two factors that govern behavior: internal and external. The law and the police are external factors. The internal factor is a personal morality. Internal factors cannot be imposed, only accepted. A well-developed moral compass should be honed. Evil exerts a barbaric and material power on millions of individuals in our society. The ferocity of frustrated instinct may be spilled upon you. Only then do you react with deadly force.

No education is complete if it does not stress certain moral and ethical values in the student. I hope to do so in these pages.

From the third edition of *Criminal Law Today: An Introduction with Capstone Cases* by Frank Schmalleger, PhD:

> Conduct that violates the law may be justifiable. A person who kills another in self-defense, for example, may be completely innocent of criminal homicide.

Reasons for innocence include necessity, self-defense, defense of others, and defense of home and property. Necessity forms the basis of all justifications. What is moral is a higher standard than what is legal, and the moral standard is the better. As an example, when we practice we must always consider decision-making. The person should be the determiner for the shot that is fired, not the weapon in their hand. That weapon might be an air gun, and the person may be a child. The person holding the gun may be an off-duty peace officer. It is the action of the individual that makes them dangerous. Unfortunately, peace officers in the metropolis shoot and wound each other on a regular basis despite good training. These are mistaken-identity shootings. Spouses have also shot each other by mistake as a product of fear or mistaken identity. My grandfather related such a case that traumatized both sides of the family when a local shopkeeper accidentally shot his wife around 1921. The primary fighting tool is the mind. Always be aware that the decision to shoot is a conscious one. There is a lot to consider, and none of the criteria may be taken lightly. When you take responsibility for your own actions, you become a citizen rather than a subject.

When training many diverse individuals, I have learned that you cannot generalize from the average performance. Each person is an individual. Just the same, there are standards I will set forth that will be an aid in development. Unlike trainers that may lower standards to adapt to a class, I cannot do so. The standard of proficiency isn't set by a group of unmotivated students. It is set by the capability of the adversary. As you are going through this book, resist the desire to skim through certain parts. The book is written with a goal in mind, and each chapter is dependent upon the previous chapter; certain goals, such as safe handling and the presentation from concealed carry, are stressed and reinforced as the book continues. Practice, train, and maintain a fighting mindset. When you are under attack and the soul starts alert, this training will save your life and the lives of your loved ones.

A note on self correction: Criticism of performance, including studying incidents in which things were done incorrectly, isn't just faultfinding but necessity. The analysis of gunfights and battles along with the knowledge of previous generations is important. We owe much to the trainers of the past 100 years, and particularly to the National Rifle Association. Without the NRA, there would be no organized training. Remember there are those who write from experience and those who claim experience. The former group is less crowded.

CHAPTER ONE

SAFETY

While there are many types of firearms, there is only one cause of accidents. The cause is always the person using the gun. A handgun is not inherently dangerous. Well-organized training schools have excellent training records, and so do the police and military. Accidents during such training are rare. Remember, it takes less time to unload

All guns are always loaded until proven otherwise! Understand the operation of each type of handgun.

the gun and make it safe than to undergo surgery. Double- and triple-check the handgun before handling, especially when engaging in dry-fire practice. Unless, that is, you are tired of living. In that case, there is little I may offer as counsel.

I am going to outline the basic safety rules and then move to the rules that apply to tactical movement. The basic safety rules will suffice for every

The revolver is simple to unload: simply open the cylinder.

A self-loader must have the magazine removed and the slide locked to the rear to be in a safe condition.

situation when properly applied. You must also understand what will occur when the safety rules are ignored. The more professional and seasoned the shooter, the safer they should be. They have probably seen the results of gunfire at some time. It isn't pretty.

A rule that I have added is that you must be completely familiar with your handgun. It is an embarrassment that students show up at training classes not knowing how to load, unload, or field strip a handgun or how to make the handgun safe. But this is something NRA instructors deal with on a daily basis. Study the manual and be certain you know how the firearm operates. Take the basic handgun course offered by the National Rifle Association before attempting an advanced course. Before you can properly apply the skills covered in this book, you must understand the basics of the handgun. Know the type of action your handgun uses and how it operates.

TYPES OF HANDGUNS

Revolvers

Single-action: The hammer must be manually cocked each time the revolver is fired. A press of the trigger drops the hammer.

Double-action: The trigger both cocks and drops the hammer. Modern double-action revolvers also usually have a single-action option.

Self-loaders

Single-action: The pistol is carried cocked with the hammer to the rear and safety on. A short press of the trigger drops the hammer.

Double-action, first-shot handgun: A long press on the trigger both cocks and drops the hammer. After the

This single-action automatic pistol is properly carried hammer to the rear and safety on—cocked and locked.

first shot is fired in double-action mode, the slide recoils and cocks the hammer for subsequent shots in single-action mode. Most, but not all, double-action, first-shot handguns feature a decocker lever that safely drops the hammer without the user touching the trigger.

The double-action, first-shot handgun may be carried fully loaded with the safety off, as illustrated, or safety on.

Double-action only: The trigger features the same press for every shot. The trigger action both cocks the hammer or, more often, the firing pin or striker. Every shot is the same: a long trigger press. In most, but not all, cases, movement of the slide partially sets the striker. This results in a relatively short and manageable trigger action.

These self-loading handguns are double-action-only designs. There is no manual safety.

SAFETY RULES

The Primary Rules

1. All guns are always loaded.
2. Never point the handgun at anything you are not willing to destroy.
3. Keep the finger off the trigger until you fire.

Be certain that you are completely familiar with handling the handgun and its safety in all weather conditions, even with gloved hands.

When moving, always make certain the trigger finger is off the trigger.

MUZZLE DISCIPLINE

Keep the firearm pointed in a safe direction at all times. Never let the muzzle cover anything you are not willing to destroy.

Keep the finger off the trigger until you are ready to fire, not when you think you will fire, but when you fire.

The gun should be unloaded when not in use.

Know how the gun operates. It is important to know how to load the handgun and make it ready to fire. It is also important to know how to unload the handgun and make it safe.

Be certain the handgun is safe to operate; an older or well-worn handgun is seldom a good idea to purchase for personal defense. Be certain the handgun is in proper working order and the safety features work as designed.

Use the correct ammunition. There are some pretty stupid ideas that are floated around the web concerning ammunition. Just because it fits the chamber doesn't mean it is safe.

These handguns seem identical, but they are chambered for different cartridges.

Be familiar with the action. This magazine is being slapped home.

The single-action handgun (top) is carried cocked and locked, while the double-action, first-shot handgun (bottom), is at ready with the hammer down and trigger forward.

Be certain that you are familiar with the operating controls of the chosen handgun. This SIG features (left to right) a magazine release, decocker, and slide lock.

Practice safety during movement. Humans are bilaterally symmetrical. We have two sides. If you are moving with the handgun, always keep the finger off the trigger. If you have the trigger finger in register, and slip and use the nondominant hand to catch yourself, you cannot avoid a clutch in the firing hand. The trigger finger will convulse in a sympathetic reaction. I have conducted simple experiments with the handgun at ready on the range and the finger on the trigger and off the trigger. When the whistle is blown, the difference in speed between beginning with the trigger finger in register and off the trigger is nonexistent, but the difference in safety is profound.

The Glock features a safety lever set in the trigger face.

Know your target. There are worse things than being shot, and one of these is shooting the wrong person. Be certain of the target, and be certain you have identified the threat. When practicing on the firing range, know your target, know what type of rounds the backstop will stop, and know what is beyond the target.

The revolver is simple to load and make safe, but do not become complacent with any handgun.

The manual of arms of different types of personal-defense handguns follows. There are many handguns, but this lexicon covers the majority. It is your responsibility to completely understand the operation of your personal handgun.

Double-Action Revolver Manual of Arms

- Operate cylinder latch and open cylinder.
- Load. Close cylinder.
- Holster. Draw. Fire.

Single-Action Self-Loader Manual of Arms

- Draw slide to the rear and lock it open.
- Insert a loaded magazine.
- Lower the slide.
- Apply the safety.
- Holster.
- Draw, disengage safety, fire.

The SIG P220 with the magazine removed.

Double-Action, First-Shot Self-Loader Manual of Arms

- Draw the slide to the rear and lock it open.
- Insert a loaded magazine.
- Lower the slide.
- Decock the hammer.
- Holster. Draw. Fire.

The SIG P220 with the magazine and round in the chamber removed; it is now safe.

Double-Action-Only Self-Loader Manual of Arms

- Draw the slide to the rear; lock it in place.
- Insert a loaded magazine.
- Lower the slide.
- Holster.
- Draw; fire.

Modify the above manual of arms as needed. Some double-action-only handguns have a manual safety; most do not. Some double-action, first-shot handguns do not have a manual safety. The CZ 75 in most variations is a double-action, first-shot handgun without a decocker, but the CZ 75 in its original form features a manual safety. Know your handgun well!

UNLOADING THE HANDGUN

The handgun is pointed in a safe direction.

Revolver: The cylinder release is pressed in the proper direction: forward for Smith and Wesson, to the rear for the Colt, and inward for Ruger. The cylinder is swung out. The muzzle is pointed upward, and the ejector rod is pushed. The cartridges should fall out. Loaded, unfired cartridge cases generally slide out of the cylinder without using the ejector rod.

Self-Loader: The magazine release is pressed, and the magazine removed. The nondominant hand racks the slide to the rear. The firing thumb locks the slide lock in place. The cartridge has been ejected and will be retrieved. The best program is to cant the slide of the handgun and allow the chambered cartridge to be ejected onto the shooting bench or a desk. After the slide is locked to the rear, insert the forefinger into the chamber to be certain there is no cartridge in the chamber. Visually check the magazine well to be certain that there is no magazine in the handgun.

When drawing or holstering the handgun, be certain that the finger does not contact the trigger.

HOLSTER SAFETY

A number of accidental discharges occur each year in holstering the handgun. The cause of the discharge is that at some point during drawing or holstering the gun, the trigger finger or part of the holster or clothing contacts the trigger and fires the weapon. With the revolver and double-action type self-loaders, it is possible to snag the trigger and fire the handgun. This has happened during holstering when a safety strap has interfered with the handgun's trigger, and in one well-documented incident, part of an officer's jacket snagged the holster and caught the trigger mechanism. The result was a leg shot. When holstering, be certain the trigger finger is away from the trigger. If not, as the gun is holstered, the trigger finger will be forced against the trigger and fire the handgun. When drawing the handgun, the trigger finger must not contact the trigger until the handgun is on target and the decision has been made to fire.

Holster safety is vital to successful critical training!

On the draw, the author keeps the trigger finger out of register with the trigger face.

CLASS SAFETY RULES

I have attended classes in which safety rules were broken. On one occasion, the instructor stood in front of the student as the student dry fired to test his control of trigger action. The instructor normally stands to one side. This young instructor noted he was "very experienced." When you see such behavior, do not walk—run—from the class. No NRA-certified instructor will behave in this manner and retain his credentials. While some shooters seem to thrive on an unwarranted cult of ego, there is no aristocracy among shooters. Grandness rests with a man in a simple house who understands his craft.

I have also heard of, but not personally experienced, reports of a class in which the students were asked to stand near a target while the instructor fired on the target, to acclimate them to being shot at! I suppose this is the civilian equivalent of crawling under barbed wire while the army instructor fires a machine gun over the soldier's head. This is necessary for a military man. At home, such foolishness must be avoided. It is difficult enough to teach basic gunhandling in a day or two; such nonstandard and dangerous procedures are not trainin, they are grandstanding.

CHAPTER TWO

GROUPS WILL NOT SAVE YOUR LIFE

Gunfights are dynamic! People move. If the assailant closes the distance, he can hurt you. Pulling the trigger until you are no longer afraid is a tactic that most understand, but this is far from an acceptable plan of action. When I began working up the details of this book, I did not simply look into my past training programs. I attempted to learn new things and be doubly certain my beliefs were correct. One fact remains constant: shooting small groups will not save your life.

Firing quickly at close range is a good gauge of skill for beginners.

Target shooting is where we all begin to learn the basics of marksmanship, but we must move past those basics. The popular press relies upon firing groups to gauge the accuracy of a handgun and compare similar handguns to each other. This is all fine for comparison, as it does speak to us concerning barrel fitting and quality of construction. But combat shooting doesn't revolve around firing small groups. The only shot that is really important is the shot you are firing at the moment. Every string of fire should be considered a series of controlled shots, with each shot intended to hit the target. I am not advocating a lower standard of accuracy, "combat accurate" as some may say. I am advocating a far higher standard of accuracy. Every shot is a singular event that must hit the target and hit the target in the right place. Firing a group for an average isn't as impressive as hitting the target on demand.

In this image, a student has produced good results with the snub-nosed .357 Magnum revolver.

This student is demonstrating excellent control with the .45 automatic.

You should practice consistently in dry fire, cling to sound principles on the range, and continue to learn close-quarters techniques. Defensive shootings are unpredictable. Our training should be flexible. The shooting skills we possess must be effective in low light, at close range, at moderate range, from behind cover, and when moving. If you cannot quickly address the target in a range setting, you will never succeed in a defensive situation against a motivated adversary. For peace officers, the shooting technique they have learned must work in uniform and from concealed carry. Likewise, the shooting technique for civilians and home-defense shooters must be consistent. You must develop skills, and in doing so, you must develop a fighting system that is both flexible and effective.

The primary focus on learning any drill is getting the firearm into the firing position. You must practice drawing the handgun from concealed carry. You must do so effortlessly without taking your eyes from the threat. Threats move, and taking your eyes away could mean they disappear from your vision. They may take cover or move into an advantageous firing position.

Training for any task is goal-oriented. You do not go to college without a plan, without the eye on a degree. You do not study haphazardly. By the same token, when you work out at the gym, you have a certain goal in mind and do not simply wander from one machine to

When practicing, it takes a lot of ammunition to maintain proficiency; make every shot count with good practice skills.

the other. You must not only have a training plan in place, you must have a means by which to measure progress. You should not simply travel to the range to make brass. While firing the handgun may build familiarity, you should be practicing a skill that is needed for personal defense.

A cornerstone of marksmanship is dry fire. Begin with a triple-checked, unloaded firearm. (And check the firearm every time you lay it down!) Dry fire doesn't cost anything and may be practiced in the home.

Always aim toward a backstop that would stop a bullet—just in case. You must be consistent in controlling the trigger. Your body will acclimate to the shooting stances and the muscles needed to control the handgun and the trigger.

The author is practicing firing with the "wrong hand."

You are practicing only one aspect of marksmanship, and that is the trigger action—although you should incidentally control the sights as well.

Let's get one fact out of the way—you cannot duplicate the stress and horror of combat on the range. The New York State Police once had a program in which officers ran 100 yards before firing and also used a "smoke house." As a young officer reading of this training, I was impressed. No doubt their present-day training is even more advanced. If you take competition seriously, IDPA (International Defensive Pistol Association) matches are an excellent training field. The point is you can practice,

With a firm, solid grip and attention to the sights, this shooter is homing in on the target.

but you cannot replicate adrenaline-dump constriction of the pupils and auditory exclusion, all of which occur during a gun battle.

Another point to consider: Your body will behave differently in one incident than another, depending upon the stress level, the toll the day has taken on you, and perhaps even the amount of coffee you have put away. A drunkard who is panhandling is bothersome, but an armed team is a deadly threat. That is why you need to get into a persistent training program. You will fight as you have trained. You may not be able to predict the problem beforehand, but you will fight well if you have trained well.

If you mix up your disciplines during training, you will revert to the simplest program during a gunfight, because your

With the handgun in recoil and a case in the air, this instructor demonstrates excellent control.

body tells you it is the easiest. I do not mean that you should not practice different drills. When you are firing at close range or long range, firing at

multiple targets, or firing in a failure-to-stop drill, always use your sights, the same sight picture, the same trigger press, and the same grip. Maintain consistency. If you sometimes fire with one hand or sometimes point the gun rather than aim, you may revert to this type of shooting at the wrong time.

Use the discipline that supplies hits and stick with it. The shots that miss are shots that are wild in the community or even among your

The presentation from the holster must be practiced and mastered before you may claim combat ability.

family. As one great gunner of the past said, "Speed's fine but accuracy is final." I cannot agree more. Work to achieve accuracy first; then work with speed. Speed isn't something miraculous that occurs one day. It is the result of the proper implementation of technique that results in the elimination of excess movement.

Affirming the grip as you draw eliminates fumbling with the grip and readjusting your hold on the handgun during movement. Executing the presentation from concealed carry with a minimum of movement results in

This student is progressing well; note the well-defined muscle in her arm as she grips the handgun.

The firing grip is a cornerstone of combat ability. Rapidly presenting the handgun into the firing grip must be mastered.

greater speed. Quickly achieving the sight picture and sight alignment, and applying the trigger press consistently each time you fire results in less jerking of the trigger and misalignment. Hits are achieved and so is speed. However, there are several rules that must be followed at all times as your training progresses.

SAFETY FIRST

Accuracy is always more important than speed. If you must slow down to get consistent hits, do so. But work on speed-building exercises. Speed is the elimination of uneconomical motion. The cadence of fire is not set by how quickly you are able to press the trigger but by how quickly you are able to recover the sight picture after recoil. The only shot that is important is the one you are firing. Do not endlessly repeat only the drills you are good at. Attempt the most challenging drills.

Do not get too complicated. Study one stance. If you find the isosceles fits your needs best, then adopt that stance. I began with the Weaver stance and still find myself using it; it would be difficult to change. Adopt, not adapt, and use the

The author is firing with the Weaver stance, one arm acting as shock absorber.

stance that works best for you. Give each an honest try and then use it at every firing session. Once you realize that target shooting will not save your life, you are ready to address the real issues.

Firing from the Weaver stance, using cover.

CHAPTER THREE

THE BEGINNER'S KIT

TOOLS AND SKILLS MUST EACH BE IN PLACE

Handgun marksmanship is challenging. This discipline is more challenging than learning to use a rifle or shotgun well. A long gun has four points of contact: the support hand, the cheek, the shoulder, and the firing hand. With the handgun, you have one or two points of contact,

This is a range bag that includes both hearing and eye protection, a tool kit, and firearms lubricant.

depending on the one- or two-hand hold, not to mention the short sight radius. The handgun is designed to save your life at relatively short range. It is all about handling and speed. Bringing the handgun into action is more challenging than working with a long gun. You must move quickly and not cover your body with the muzzle. Developing speed in presenting the firearm for action must be coupled with the ability to deliver accurate fire with the most difficult of all firearms to master. You must have the proper mindset. You would not shoot clay birds with a scope-mounted rifle or attempt to engage a 200-yard target with a buckshot-loaded shotgun. Understand the capabilities of the handgun.

In order for training to proceed smoothly, with minimal interruption, you must put together a range bag. Most ranges have rules concerning carrying the gun to the range. It must be in a container of some type. Some allow a holstered handgun that is locked open. The range bag provides a carrier. The range bag should include these items at a minimum:

Hearing protection in the form of effective, muff-type devices, not ear plugs.

Extra pair of hearing muffs.

Shooting glasses. They may be clear or tinted. Never proceed without hearing and eye protection. You will be barred from a reputable range. You

Hearing and eye protection is a must for range work.

may damage your hearing. You may lose your eyesight. Always wear these important devices! Time spent with older instructors that are forced to yell at each other in normal conversation is motivation enough for hearing protection.

A tool for adjusting the sights. If your sights are the screw-type, adjustable units, the pistol may have come with this tool.

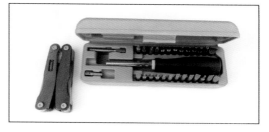

Spare magazines for the pistol. Three is a minimum. One in the gun, one for carry, and one resting. You should obtain and use a minimum of five

The Caspian 1911 tool (left) and the tool kit from Cheaperthandirt.com (right) get a lot of use on the firing range.

magazines once you have decided upon the pistol you will carry. Simple readiness demands this. Range time goes much more smoothly with a good supply of quality magazines.

The magazines that are used with the handgun should be manufactured by the maker of the handgun: SIG for SIG, Beretta for Beretta. An exception is the giant maker Mec-Gar, as they actually manufacture most of the magazines supplied with European-quality handguns. With the 1911, factory-quality magazines are a must. Ed Brown custom magazines are ideal.

Good-quality magazines are essential for firearms practice.

Brownells seven- and eight-round magazines are an excellent option. The D and L Sports magazine is a good product.

Please do not show up at a training class with only one magazine. Taking time to load that single magazine holds up everyone on the range and is also the mark of an amateur. It is particularly embarrassing if you do have spare magazines and have left them at home.

HPR ammunition has given excellent results, at a fair price, in training.

A supply of ammunition for the handgun. If you are firing more than one handgun at the range, and they are different calibers, be certain that the ammunition is separated and remains separated. A number of blowups have occurred by mixing ammunition. Likewise, the ammunition should be of good quality and appropriate for the task at hand. When beginning, factory ball ammunition of proven quality is a must. Black Hills Ammunition, Fiocchi, HPR, and Winchester Ammunition are among the best choices for practice ammunition. Quality ammunition is important when proofing the handgun. Handloads or ammunition of unknown quality will confuse the issue when you are testing the handgun.

Lubricating oil for the handgun.

A minimal cleaning kit.

Headgear for protection from the sun.

Water, if the range trip is extended.

A proper holster. Range holsters are good for beginners; at a later date, you will progress to practice with carry gear.

Two places are likely to have everything you need: Brownells.com and Cheaperthandirt.com work for me. A drive to Cabela's is always pleasant as well.

The SIG P220 is carried in a Barber Chameleon, a suitable range holster.

BAD HABITS

In handgun marksmanship, we walk before we can run. It is vital that we learn the correct operation of the handgun and proper marksmanship first. If we pick up bad habits, they are difficult to dispense with. As an example, I worked with a student who was a good shot but hopelessly slow and prone to fumble when preparing to shoot. He was using his weak hand to manipulate the safety, slide stop, and magazine release of his handgun! I was surprised when he told me he had attended a class that taught him to use the weak hand for manipulation. You do not always have two hands available, but such manipulation as he attempted was painfully slow as well. It is a shame that some develop such backward rubbish and manage to teach others the same. I cannot understand how such folks come up with such wrong-headed ideas and then manage to propagate them. In another case, a trainer came up with an alternate firing stance for use in buildings. The stance canted the handgun to one side and was stable, but effectively blocked the student's vision to one side. As I have often mentioned, master the conventional before attempting to invent something that, in all likelihood, has been invented and discarded a hundred years ago.

The best student is a blank slate with no preconceived notions. Yet, I suspect most of you have some sort of background in firing the handgun and in practice. Carefully consider the means by which you manipulate the handgun and how your firing and marksmanship habits are affected. Along the way I am certain that you will find some habit or shortcoming that limits your marksmanship. I continually work on personal development. Since my profession demands I test many types of handguns, my own shortcomings are a fertile ground for study as I test and fire diverse firearms. Each handgun may require a slightly different grip and technique. Let's start at the beginning.

EYE DOMINANCE

A simple test early in the game will determine your eye dominance. Most of us are right-handed with a right dominant eye, but this isn't always the case. It isn't difficult to understand if we are right or left *hand* dominant; we are exhibiting traits by the time we reach our first birthday. Eye dominance is another matter.

It is simple enough to learn which eye is dominant. With both eyes open, focus on an object across the room, such as a clock or doorknob. Bring the arms to full extension and have the hands meet in the line of sight. You should form a triangle with the thumbs of each hand. Place the object you wish to view in the middle of the open triangle

This student is checking for eye dominance.

formed by the thumbs. With both eyes open, the object will be clear. Close one eye and the other alternately. When the object in view is covered by the hand as you close one eye, the other eye is the dominant eye. If you close the left eye, and the object remains visible, as an example, you are right-eye dominant. If you are left-eye dominant and right-handed, it is not a major problem. It is simple enough to use the left eye for sighting a right-handed gun stance, provided the proper techniques are used. Remember, we hold the head erect and bring the gun to the eyes; we do not hold the gun in the hand and then scrunch the head down to meet the gun. If the neck is compressed, blood flow to the eyes may be compromised. The result is blurred vision. With the head and shoulders in the proper firing position, it isn't difficult to fire with one eye and the other hand.

TRAINING MUST PROGRESS TO THE FOLLOWING SKILLS

- Learning to safely handle the firearm.
- Learning to load and unload the firearm.
- Learning to fire accurately.
- Learning to shoot quickly.
- Learning to present the handgun from a concealed-carry holster.
- Learning to address multiple targets.
- Learning to fire while moving and to address moving targets.

THE FIRING GRIP

The firing grip must control recoil, allow easy manipulation of the controls and the trigger, and also present the handgun naturally toward the target. A lot of time is lost if the handgun isn't smoothly presented into the firing position. After the trigger is pressed and the pistol fires, we wish to control the pistol and return the sights to the same position for shot after shot.

When firing rapidly off hand, a steady firing position is mandatory.

This type of control is firmly invested in the grip. The firing grip should stand on its own and not be related to the stance. If you are firing from the Isosceles or the Weaver stance, firing upright, firing from cover, firing from prone, or even when moving, the grip is independent and does not rely upon the arms. The grip should be as strong as possible. If the grip is too relaxed, the pistol will not be properly controlled in recoil. If the grip isn't firm, a self-loader may not properly function. The action may short cycle. When practicing with light loads or even the .22 rimfire handgun, I maintain the same strong grip as if I were firing my .45 Auto or .44 Special revolver. This is simply good procedure and builds confidence in the proper grip.

When gripping the handgun, the hand should be as high on the handgun and the backstrap as possible. The support fingers wrap around the front strap and apply pressure straight to the rear. Lateral pressure will cause misalignment. The double-action revolver must be stabilized for proper trigger control, and the self-loader must be stabilized to function properly. The trigger finger is angled in to lay on the face of the trigger for firing. The trigger finger must not mash the trigger to one side or the other. The

This student is beginning with a relaxed stance, learning the basics.

fingers of the firing hand must not move in sympathetic motion as the trigger finger presses the trigger. This is called milking the grip and will destroy accuracy. To determine your proper, strongest grip, squeeze the handgun as tightly as possible until your hand begins to tremble. Then ease off pressure, and you have your proper grip. The pressure on the fingers must be equal.

The two-hand hold is essential for the best control and for rapid-fire marksmanship. The support hand wraps around the firing hand, and the

upper digit of the support hand will be hard against the bottom of the trigger guard. There is no point in wrapping the forefinger of the support hand against the front of the trigger guard. This breaks up the integrity of the grip. In the proper firing grip, the firing hand fingers will be curled together and supported by the heel of the support hand. The competitor's

When beginning, recoil control seems a chore. This student proceeded from the 9mm to the .45 in time.

grip is a grip in which the support hand supplies most of the pressure. This is a comfortable grip, useful in long competitions and for target shooting. This isn't the ideal firing grip for personal defense. The strongest possible grip should be maintained for combat shooting. As a rule, the strong, thumbs-forward grip style works best for the majority of shooters. The strong side thumb lies over the support thumb. They are not interlocked but support each other.

Some experimentation is needed to find the ideal firing grip and thumb position for the individual. As an example, the strong, thumbs-forward grip may interfere with the rotation of the cylinder in a revolver if the thumbs are long enough. A grip with the thumbs held higher would be indicated. Avoid the firing grip with the support thumb wrapped around the joint of the firing-hand thumb. The slide of the self-loading pistol will recoil and cut into the thumb if you practice this grip. With the revolver, this grip is also less than ideal. The grip must be consistently applied. If you allow the fingers of the support hand to be loosened by recoil, they may fly into the magazine release or the slide lock. The thumb-into-the-slide-lock malfunction is among the most common shooter-induced malfunctions.

Some handguns are more difficult to grip properly than others. Consider this fact when choosing a defensive firearm. Hand fit is important. If you cannot hold the firearm in a normal firing grip with the hand high on the backstrap and the first pad of the finger on the trigger, the handgun may be too large for your hand. If the hand must be canted into an H-type grip, the handgun is too large.

LOCKING THE WRIST

The wrist must be locked to control the handgun. When you are striving to get the hands as high on the pistol as possible, the wrist should move the heel of the support hand as high and flat as possible. The thumbs should never ride the side of the gun. By the same token, if the trigger finger contacts the handgun, except on the trigger, the end result is pressing against the frame when you press the trigger. This means you are adding weight and inconsistency to the trigger press.

Firing the .45 Automatic, this student demonstrates the proper grip and good control.

When achieving the proper grip, it is best to think not right and left hand but rear and forward hand and apply equal pressure. It is a physiological fact that the dominant hand is stronger than the nondominant hand. We have to achieve the strongest-possible grip while understanding these factors. There are opposite and equal actions that take place when the firearm discharges. The muzzle rises during recoil. The backstrap moves to the rear while the front strap rises. These forces must be controlled.

The wrist is a big part of this control and so is the support hand. The proper technique is exactly why some feel that the 1911 .45 is controllable and comfortable to fire and others find the piece a challenge. The wrist keeps the hands solid. The support hand keeps the firing hand from moving. By extension, the handgun does not move to a great degree. Controlling the handgun boils down to returning it to the position it was in before the handgun fired. A proper grip will ensure that there is less interference with the aim and recovery. The rifleman has four points of contact: the shoulder, cheek, forward support hand, and firing hand. The handgunner has only one point of contact. We should have as much contact with the handgun as possible and this should be in the form of a two-hand grip that is both strong and geometrically correct. The handgun is

Note this student is controlling his Springfield Mil Spec .45 as it cycles.

held with both side-to-side pressure—primarily from the support hand—and front-to-rear pressure with the firing hand.

In close-range combat, two hands are used (unless the support hand is disabled), period. The other reason for firing with one hand is firing from the retention position. I have done any number of personal experiments and conducted drills with students of varying ability. Drawing and moving to the two-hand firing position is the fastest and most accurate, with an advantage in speed of as much as 25 percent and much greater accuracy. You should practice one-hand fire occasionally and be able to make hits with one

hand at modest range if necessary. If you have time to practice, one-hand fire is challenging at longer range and builds skill. But those who move into the solid two-hand hold have less waver in the grip. Do not simply take my advice on this, although it is well researched. Practice quickly drawing and moving to the two-hand grip. Fire at a target at the seven-yard line. Next, practice drawing into the one-

This student prefers the double-action-only SIG and is learning to master the long-but-smooth trigger action.

hand grip and repeat the drill. As you will see, the two-hand grip is not only rock steady in comparison but as fast or faster than stabilizing the handgun with one hand. The firing grip must be affirmed as the handgun is grasped in the holster.

The retention position is considered an extension of the draw. The handgun is drawn from the holster and then positioned on your side. The elbow shoots to the rear to draw the handgun, and then the elbow drops to bring the handgun into the retention position. At very close range when you are under attack by a blunt weapon, an edged weapon, or a firearm thrust into the body, the retention position is a lifesaver. The firing grip must be strong and the muscles in the arm as tight as possible. The firmness of the position ensures that you will control the firearm and that the firearm will cycle when fired. Bringing the arm close to the body to amplify the grip is similar to bringing a stubborn jar lid close to the body to amplify power. You should have a great deal of gripping power with the retention position.

To execute the retention position, the pistol is drawn and moved into position. The support-side hand is drawn well out of the way. The body is crouched on the rear foot for support. At this range, you may be under physical attack, and you do not wish to be knocked over. The foot to the rear supports the body. Fire two rounds for each repetition. As you become familiar with the drill, move to protecting the head and neck with the support hand and firing as you do so.

TRIGGER COMPRESSION

Controlling the trigger is a cornerstone of marksmanship and among the most difficult skills. Trigger control is vital to hitting the target. If sight picture and sight alignment are not perfect at close range, but the trigger press is, you will probably get a hit. If sight alignment is perfect, but you jerk the trigger, you will miss by a mile. Well, might as well be a mile! The trigger must be pressed without allowing the sights to move out of alignment. The goal is not to jerk the trigger but to press the trigger. Even when you are firing rapidly, the trigger press is the same: to the rear and smooth. Some action types, such as the double-action, first-shot handgun, demand the trigger finger reach in an arc and then down to press the trigger, and then you make a transition to the single-action, press. Complicated, and perhaps unnecessarily so, but many shooters do well with this type of action.

For pure accuracy, a surprise break is preferred. This means that the trigger is pressed, and when the shot breaks, you know it is coming, but you do not have time to flinch in anticipation of the shot. There are highly experienced shooters who claim they know exactly when the shot will break. They are also fine shots. If you reach that level, the knowledge of the moment the shot breaks may be realized.

Some try to ambush the trigger and jerk it at the right moment. This doesn't work. Others cannot confirm the sight picture and fight the front sight, wandering across the target. They have taken too long to get the proper sight picture, seem to find it on target, and quickly jerk the trigger. This leads to a miss. There is a difference between trigger control for accuracy and trigger control for accurate control in close-quarters battle, which I will discuss in the chapter on close-quarters combat.

Some shooters anticipate recoil. This leads to the involuntary muscle contraction known as flinch. Flinch also ruins the trigger press. Dry-fire practice will combat flinch, so will moving to the .22-caliber handgun for a few practice runs. It is important to place the first digit of the trigger finger directly on the trigger face, press straight to the rear, and control the trigger. When you press the trigger and the gun fires, the trigger will reset. Allow the trigger to reset; do not ride the trigger. Press, reset, press, reset is the cadence. Dry-fire practice is essential to building skill with the handgun, and this is very important in mastering the trigger action. The slow press of the target shooter may not be applicable to combat shooting, but you always deliver a press, not a quick jerk. It is equally important to allow time for the trigger action to reset. In extreme cases of using improper trigger control, the handgun will fail to reset, and the pistol will not fire again.

MARKSMANSHIP

Marksmanship is simply directing the path of the bullet. It isn't an arcane art but a science. The point of impact on the target is controlled by the point of aim of the sights. All handgun sights rely upon the same principle. Target pistols may feature high-profile sights with a fine sight picture. Combat handguns may have low-profile sights that are designed to be snag proof. All require the same type of alignment. There are two important steps. A practiced shooter will execute both at the same time. These are sight alignment and sight picture.

There are different types of front sights. As a general rule, the higher visibility, the better.

The skills are more important than the hardware, and that is why we will discuss the procedure to obtain proficiency at arms before we discuss the actual arms. The goal is to hit the target—not to make covering fire and not to fire a warning shot or anything of that nature. The only moral goal is to hit the target. Only by obtaining a good grasp of the traditional marksmanship fundamentals may you apply these skills to the combat maneuvers known as tactics. The basics of marksmanship will save your life. As an NRA-certified instructor, I must chase away a number of myths and teach students to fire their handguns quickly, safely, and accurately.

A dangerous myth is the myth of point shooting or instinctive shooting. I am not going to waste time on that fallacy, except to note that I will not be the instructor who admits to a judge that I taught a student not to use their sights in a defensive encounter. If a student wounds or kills an innocent person as a result of ignoring the sights, then a jury of average citizens might conclude that I was as negligent as a driving instructor teaching students to drive with their eyes closed. Only by using the sights and sight alignment properly will you secure a hit—particularly at longer handgun ranges. There are exceptions: firing from the retention position is one, and the meat and paper drills are another; but you will learn that in meat and paper we aim. The alignment of the pistol is simply nontraditional. At any range at which you can use the sights, you will, and that begins at about three yards. It is faster to move to the two-hand hold and use the sights, as you will see. Advocating a point-shooting system in which the handgun is aimed by "feel" without regard to the sights is cavalier at best and unprofessional.

SIGHT ALIGNMENT

Sight alignment is simple enough, as far as the geometry goes. The front sight is either a post or a blade attached to the slide or the barrel of the handgun. The rear sight is an open sight with raised bars or posts on each side. The sight radius is the distance between the two sights. Within reason, the longer the sight radius, the easier it is to achieve a perfect sight picture. The shorter sight radius of compact pistols and the snub-nosed .38 exaggerates mistakes in alignment. Particular care must be taken with these handguns.

To hit the target, simply align the front post between the rear posts in the rear notch with an equal amount of light on each side of the post. The top of the front sight should be equal with the tops of each rear leaf. Sight alignment is a constant whether or not you have an object in your sights. The balance between front and rear sight and sight alignment cannot be compromised. You may practice sight alignment in dry fire. Mistakes in sight alignment are magnified by the distance between the shooter and the target.

This is the proper sight alignment; the sight picture is also good.

Sight picture is the superimposition of the sights on the target. You must hold the sight alignment true while the sights are placed on the object you must strike with a bullet. Because we are practicing for defensive shooting, we begin facing a one-dimensional target we are squared to. I primarily use the Birchwood Casey B-27 Eze-Score Target, and with the orange center, the beginner will find the target offers good contrast with the sights. By beginning with a three-dimensional target you are squared to, you may advance to more challenging targets and scenarios.

Keep the sights aligned properly and place the front sight directly under the X-ring of the target for the "six o'clock" hold and dead on the target for the "dead-on" hold. Holding under the target in the six o'clock hold is most common, and most combat handguns are regulated for this hold. The premise is that a pistol regulated to strike slightly high at close range gives you a fighting chance to hit the target at fifty yards. Handguns differ, and you must confirm your sight regulation.

The most important point is that you impose the sight alignment over the target, resulting in sight picture. You cannot aim for an area; you must aim for a small part of the target. As an example, a person debriefed after a gunfight often says they aimed for a certain part of the adversary's clothing, such as a shirt button. They have hit the target. Those who miss have aimed for the whole body. Aim for a small part of the target, and the bullet will do the most good. Center mass as an aiming point is misunderstood. The correct aiming point in combat is often defined as the arterial region of the heart. This is the only area other than the cranial vault that is likely to give a rapid shutdown of the system with a single round from a powerful handgun. But the adversary will not always be squared to the shooter. He may be running at you, bladed to you as he fires, or behind cover. The center of mass is the center of the target that is presented. If the shoulder is presented, then the center of the shoulder is the center of mass. If the hip and a leg are exposed from cover, the center of the exposed hip or leg is the target. By firing at the center of the mass exposed, you have a good chance of striking the target.

SIGHT FOCUS

The front sight should be sharp and clear with the proper sight focus. The rear sight and the target will each be blurred. It is all about the front sight—FRONT SIGHT, FRONT SIGHT, FRONT SIGHT. If you are in a low-light situation and the only sighting choice you have is the front sight, then you will superimpose the front sight on the lower section of the threat. With the front sight held higher than normal for visibility at close range, the bullets will

This Glock features Trijicon night sights, the preferred option for Glock shooters.

strike a bit high if you aim using only the front sight; put the front sight on the belt buckle, and the bullets will go into the abdominal area. This is a modification of the standard sight picture that also works well for combat shooting.

Accuracy is always more important than speed. Speed is simply mastering economy of motion. Practice, and practice well, and speed comes. The cadence of fire will never be dictated by how quickly you can pull the trigger. I am pretty certain I could teach a monkey to pull the trigger quickly. Press the trigger, allow the rear sight and the target to blur, and concentrate on the front sight.

The cadence of fire is set by how quickly you recover the sights after recoil. When practicing, convince yourself that only the shot being fired is important. Follow up shots, if needed, take care of themselves. Do not fire strings but a series of controlled shots with attention to the trigger press, sight alignment, and sight picture with each shot. No matter how quickly you fire, the cadence of fire is not set by how quickly you press the trigger; it is determined by how quickly you realign your sights on the target after each shot.

Maintaining the sight picture and sight alignment while firing is the secret of accurate shooting at any range. Press the trigger straight to the rear with no deviation or mashing of the trigger. You will hit the target every time. You cannot hold the pistol rock steady, but there is movement that doesn't matter as much as misalignment of the sights. If you have alignment—the front blade is centered—there may be some lateral and horizontal wobble but you will still strike the target. Let's agree that the vital area of the target—the human torso—is about four inches wide. When you practice in slow fire at seven yards, you may have a bit of wobble and still fire five rounds into one ragged hole. Concentrate on alignment, and wobble will take care of itself. Wobble, arm sway, and body sway all degrade accuracy, but the practiced combat shooter doesn't let them cause a missed shot.

FOLLOW-THROUGH

A ball player continues his swing after he hits the ball, and a golfer does not release his grip after he contacts the golf ball. What you do after you fire could impact what you do before you release the grip. Keep the handgun held tightly, and do not relax the grip. This ensures proper recoil function, ejecting one case and loading another. It also keeps your grip and accuracy consistent. You will lose your image of the front sight for a brief interval, and with the proper grip, you quickly will realign the sights and get back on target.

Follow-through is essential for controlling the firearm:

1. Keep the grip.
2. Allow the trigger to reset.
3. Maintain the sight picture.
4. A consistent grip allows repeatability of accurate fire.

Each shot is a controlled, singular event. Do not consider a firing string to be a volley of shots; rather, consider each shot as the most important shot. That is the key to hitting the target. Shooting without the desire and ability to hit is nonsense. Each shot is independent; only a machine gun will cover the target in bullets. A handgun cannot be fired quickly enough to use machine-gun tactics, such as the figure eight or shooting through a target. You must make each shot count.

CENTER OF MASS

If you aim for the center of mass to stop a fight, it is not always as you perceive it. The center of mass is sometimes perceived as the area between the shoulders, with the heart as the center. The center of mass, in mathematical terms, is an axis of symmetry and constant density. In combat shooting, the center of mass is the center of the target. That means that if there is only a shoulder or a leg exposed, you will fire for the center of that mass. If you are trying to align a perfect shot to the arterial region of the heart, you are going to hold your fire a long time. The center of an exposed target is the center of mass. If the head is the only target, as in a case in which the opponent is firing around a corner, then you aim for the center of the cranium. If your adversary is kneeling and firing around cover with a kneecap exposed, then you fire at the center of the knee. Whatever the target, aiming for the geometric center is the proper aiming point, allowing the greatest chance of a hit. In the unlikely event you have the perfect shot at a threat facing and squared to you, *then* the center of the chest is the best target.

Do not rely on that perfect shot, and always aim for the center of mass—whatever that center might be.

REVIEW

- Your stance should be rock solid.
- You should stand with your feet about shoulder width apart.
- Stand with your feet at about a forty-five-degree angle toward the target, not flat-footed.
- Your weight should be well distributed.
- You should lean into the gun.
- Your arms are simply thrust out with the Isosceles stance. With the Weaver stance, you keep one arm straight and slightly bend your support arm. Square your body to the target with the Isosceles stance, but with the Weaver stance, your body is bladed to the target. Although you can do good work with either, the Weaver is the professional's choice.

CHAPTER FOUR

A PLACE TO SHOOT

Whatever the discipline, we need training and an area to practice. Finding a suitable dojo may be easier than finding a serviceable pistol range. We must be able to train effectively, not simply punch the ten ring out of a bull's-eye target. Indoor ranges work well for the beginner and the early phases of training. We are shooting slowly and striving for safety and accuracy, both absolutes that cannot be diminished. You simply cannot jump into tactical shooting and proceed well. A well-planned layout in an outdoor or square range is far superior, in my opinion, for training compared to the indoor range.

Brittany Caton is a certified instructor. She is demonstrating the proper stance, grip, and sight alignment.

A person with intelligence and the ability to train will be able to perform many tasks reasonably well. It is akin to a liberal-arts education—pistol craft should be a versatile skill. Where pistol craft is considered, a variety of skills are essential. These skills include presentation, firing when moving, and firing at multiple targets. These skills must be practiced often. Joining the local IDPA or IPSC (International Practical Shooting Confederation) club is a great idea. Movement, accuracy, and safety are stressed. Unlike some trainers in personal defense, I see no downside to competition shooting. Of course, it isn't realistic or exactly applicable to personal defense. But it certainly gets you shooting and presents a challenge, and I think that is a good idea. The debate between personal defense shooters and competition shooters exists mostly in the pages of gun magazines. Most shooters who excel at one or the other shoot both disciplines.

Good control with the compact 9mm; note case in the air.

The range location must incorporate several important features. Safety is foremost. A backstop is essential. Bullets may ricochet, so the backstop or berm must be a good one. When you have found the right range, there are many considerations. As one example, it is essential that you maintain a means of communication. Medical conditions, such as high blood pressure, an emergency, such as heat stroke, or even a dangerous insect bite may flare up at the worst times. A minor cut may become more serious far from help. Dehydration or something as simple as a sprained ankle can cause a problem. Such considerations are important, and keeping the cell phone handy is a good safety net.

It is good to have a range buddy with you. There have been problems at public ranges, including some piece of crap stealing your guns and gear while you walk to the targets unaware of his or her lurking presence. This is less likely on a private range, where you are a member and there is a locked gate. Some of these ranges charge a fee that is very modest, considering the maintenance and insurance costs. I like to let someone in the family know I am going to the range and my approximate check-in and checkout times. A gunshot, God forbid, isn't my primary worry. The same types of problems that occur with any sport are my main concerns. These are overheating and sprained muscles. Watch the weather, and be prepared as if you were hiking or spelunking, and the rest will take care of itself if you have learned range safety. There is always an inherent danger in using a firearm. The same is true of a vehicle, a chainsaw, a wood router, or a motorcycle. I am not going to stop using a firearm or other tools, and I am going to use each tool safely.

You must be able to move and shoot on the range. You will not be firing at two-dimensional paper targets you are squared to during a real fight, so movement and a degree of realism are essential. You must find a range where you can practice effectively. The presentation may be practiced at home, but at some point when you feel safe and ready, you must proceed to the presentation and include a draw in the presentation. Move, shoot, practice. Dry-fire runs in the home have their place, but there is no substitute for live-fire exercise. An ideal range will have a large, open area for firing from ranges of 0 to 25 yards and will be surrounded on three sides by berms. (The typical rifle range has only a berm at the end of the range, downrange, and will be spaced at 50 to 200 yards.) You can work with a single berm, but the Adirondack-shape firing range design,

In this illustration, the instructor is setting up a run on targets.

open on one end and surrounded on the three sides, allows the placement of shooting areas side-by-side. The bullets and the firing berm are always away from the vicinity in which you will be firing. When a range is properly set up, you will be able to practice line of cover and movement. Always be aware that you cannot fire upward! Some of the drills, such as stopping and firing into the body in a crowd, may only be practiced dry fire. Even if I were on a desert section in Arizona without any town in sight, I would be leery of motorcyclists and hikers. So, some drills must be practiced relentlessly and others primarily by dry fire, but 99 percent of the work you do may be practiced dry fire.

Among the best training aids you will find are steel reaction targets. Hanging plates react to a good hit and also react to a bad hit; a complete miss doesn't register at all. A shot in the center sends the target reeling to the rear. If the hit is high or low, the reaction isn't the same, and this is easily observed. Only a solid, center hit will provide the desired result. A shot to the left or right will tip the target in the direction of the hit. There is instant feedback, unlike a paper target.

In fact, the steel gong is perhaps the best training aid, as concentration on an eight-inch steel plate is challenging. Also, if you attempt to use a minor caliber, you only hear a light ping, not the solid slap of a 9mm +P or .45. A fast-moving 9mm or .357 and the slow-moving .45 ACP have different timbres.

This student is practicing controlling the trigger, aligning the sights, and controlling recoil at close range.

While there are benefits to the indoor range, muzzle flash and muzzle report are sometimes amplified.

There are many lessons in shooting steel. I have also used a stand-alone steel target from InnovativeTargets.net with excellent results. The target is set up at an appropriate distance, and when fired, it swings downward and then returns to the original position. A good shot who is in control of the handgun will be able to keep the plate bouncing with hits. I also have on hand the heavy plate for the .308 rifle, so this is a versatile target well suited to many shooting disciplines.

A problem with open ranges is the possibility of inclement weather. Getting rained out after a long drive isn't pleasant. On the other hand, if the weather isn't severe, training in all conditions is important. Training when it is cold, when you are wearing winter clothing, and when you are wearing summer attire is important and should be conducted. You will learn how your ability is gauged against the demands of personal defense. The indoor range is most often set for a single temperature. You may train with covering garments, but it isn't quite the same. Jack Frost isn't nipping at your nose. For those who live in a true four-season climate, the outdoor range may be a challenge. If a firearm or support gear fails, it is better to learn of this weakness on the range.

SET
FOR
MATCH
PLEASE DO
NOT
DISTURB

When on the range, respect others, and always obey range rules.

I was reluctant when first attending a match at the indoor range, because I wasn't used to firing inside. After just a few range sessions, however, I began to enjoy the indoor range. At the time my schedule was tight, and the only allocation I had for practice was at night, so the indoor range was much appreciated. And I believe I became a more versatile shooter by attending training and matches at different ranges. At the indoor range, the pace may be slow. You will be able to fire at the target, press a button to bring the target back, and then send it downrange. Almost every indoor range features a motorized target carrier. A very few may still exist that have a rope-and-pulley arrangement for manually moving the target back and forth and bringing it to rest at different ranges. This isn't really bad. They prevent over-travel in most cases. Many of us like the convenience of an electric wire or rope-and-pulley target system. A drawback of the indoor range is that gunshots may be startling in an enclosed area, even with muffs, and there is

The outdoor range often allows flexibility in training.

DIFFERENCES BETWEEN INDOOR AND OUTDOOR RANGES

- The indoor range often has clearly marked firing lines at different ranges.
- The ranges, however, are usually shorter, with some reaching to fifteen yards, others to twenty-five yards maximum.
- The weather is always hospitable in the indoor range.
- Ammunition and targets are available at the indoor range if you run out of either or have left something at home.
- The indoor range is often open at late hours, a real boon to those of us with busy schedules.
- A mix of training at both types of ranges is often profitable.

Learning the proper grip, stance, sight alignment, and sight picture are essential to your development as a shooter.

always the guy at the next booth with the .44 Magnum. Unfortunately, the range rules at indoor ranges often prohibit drawing and firing. This goes back to the drill of performing the presentation in the dry-fire mode, which is good to a point.

RANGE DANGERS: RICOCHET

When we discuss range dangers, the primary consideration is always a bullet over the berm or one that flies unfettered without being stopped by the target or backstop. But ricochet is also a grave danger. I have personally seen the effects of ricochet and realize that ricochet can be dangerous. While scientifically predictable, ricochet is sometimes surprising. Because I spent a good bit of my adult life wearing a badge, many of the incidents I observed were in the field rather than on the range, but they are certainly applicable to the range. As just a few examples, in one incident I fired a 230-grain .45 ACP at a vehicle side glass, only to see it leave a long mark on the curve of the glass as it deflected. The angle was severe. On another occasion, a 210-grain .41 Magnum was fired into a car door at a very slight downward angle. The bullet hit the heavy seat backing of a 1960s Chrysler vehicle and bounced through the roof almost exactly perpendicular to the ground. I once investigated vehicle penetration by small arms extensively, studying every case I could find and firing into junked vehicles to satisfy my curiosity. The steel plates the FBI uses for testing are repeatable in experimentation. Actual vehicles are unpredictable. On one occasion, a bullet had entered the car door, struck a brace, and bounced back out of the door toward the shooter. In the only occasion in which I was wounded by gun fire, a bullet fragment bounced from the ground and struck my leg. I am no stranger to ricochet; you may say I have made its intimate acquaintance!

Few shooters understand ricochet and ricochet potential well. This may lead to problems for shooters, ranges, and neighbors. Bullets do not bounce like rubber balls, but deflect at an angle. You own every bullet and must take responsibility for this. Ranges must be constructed to avoid or eliminate ricochet. A fair question may be which bullets have the greatest potential for deflection? The answer is that round-nose bullets are among the most offensive. Spherical projectiles, such as buckshot, are similar. If the bullet goes into a berm, bullet shape doesn't matter. If they strike a hard surface, including the ground, the bullet shape matters a lot. This is why we seek to avoid and eliminate ground shots. Velocity is an important component of the equation. High-velocity bullets penetrate more and with proper bullet design are more likely to fragment. The single bullet type to be avoided for best safety is the RNL (Round-Nosed Lead) bullet at low velocity. But, again, it doesn't matter if the shots go into the berm.

The impacted surface is also worthy of consideration. Water is likely to produce ricochet, much like a skipping stone across the surface. Depending on the angle of incidence, almost any surface will produce a ricochet with an RNL or spherical bullet. Many of us have fired at an old fence post or hardened wood. This surface is among the few that will often produce a bounce back to the shooter. A low-velocity RNL load, such as the .32 Smith & Wesson with a 98-grain bullet at 650 fps, is particularly offensive. Up the velocity to the .32 Magnum and the bullet penetrates and doesn't bounce back. Add a JHP (Jacketed Hollow-Point) bullet, and you are in much better shape for safety.

The angle of incidence is important concerning ricochet potential. This is simply the angle at which the bullet meets the surface. A low angle of incidence produces a likely ricochet, and the angle of departure may be low, or the bullet may be sent into the air. Steel targets—the common gong—are suspended from a chain. This arrangement allows the target to give a little when the bullet meets the target, deflecting the bullet into the ground, and makes steel targets among the safest of all targets. Just the same, do not get too close, as bullet fragments are dangerous to twenty feet or more. Among the greatest dangers is when the angle of incidence and the angle of departure match. It is rare to see 180-degree refraction, but it happens. When a projectile that is stabilized by the rifling spin is subjected to certain conditions, spin is canceled. Sometimes the bullet reverses, with the base moving forward. This is known as progression, or tumbling. A bullet may even ricochet in a lateral direction, depending upon bullet spin.

The outdoor range offers more flexibility than the indoor range and is preferred for most combat drills.

There is always a loss of velocity and energy when a projectile ricochets. The bullet will be less stable after being deflected. It may even depend upon what attitude the bullet moves through the air as to the range of a ricochet. After a great deal of research into the situation, I have concluded that it is more beneficial to be concerned with a bullet that flies over the berm or leaves the range than a ricochet. Most ricochets play out quickly and are no longer dangerous within a few hundred feet. The missed round that goes over the berm, however, retains its original energy and range. The problem that should be addressed is missed shots. Short-range ricochet inside the confines of the range is more dangerous to the shooter and others on the range than long-range ricochet, per my research and experience. Ricochets may happen with any firearm but are most likely with low-velocity lead bullets. Ricochets are least likely with high-velocity frangible bullets. Plan accordingly and let safety be the guide.

CHAPTER FIVE

THE FIRST SHOTS

THE FIRST HANDGUN

Many correspondents and individuals that attend my class ask which handgun would be best for their first handgun. These are individuals with no prior experience. While I have had the privilege to train soldiers, cops, and other experienced shooters, many students are without meaningful experience. Sometimes they have a wish to learn the handgun well and have time; others need a handgun for defense right now. I have recommended that they take the class first with a rented or borrowed handgun and then make the decision. I ask if they have any prior shooting experience. Some have, but many have never fired a handgun. The majority of new handgunners are interested in personal defense. Others have a wide variety of interests, and the handgun is simply a passing fad with them.

A poorly chosen handgun will defeat the purpose of learning to use the handgun well. A .40-caliber compact pistol or small-frame .357 Magnum revolver is not the best first choice. Recoil is too much even for many accomplished shooters. A handgun that is relatively simple to operate is indicated as a first handgun. An inexpensive handgun is okay, but a cheap handgun is not. Pride of ownership and good function are encouraging aspects of the handgunning game. A poorly made or troublesome handgun will be discouraging to a beginner and limit his or her practice. Buy quality, and you will never regret the decision. Many beginners move up a notch soon after the initial purchase to a handgun better suited to their needs. Others find handguns interesting and discover that multiple handguns are required to meet their needs and interests. Many of us come to own handguns we never intended for serious use but that are interesting. Focus on the personal-defense handgun and training with this handgun. Once the most important niche in your handgun battery is filled, you

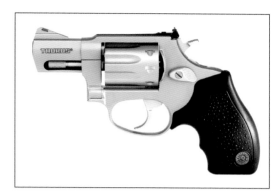

A quality double-action revolver in .22 caliber is a great learning tool.

may add those that interest you. Do not become distracted from the task at hand.

For those with time and effort to invest in the training scenario, a .22-caliber double action revolver is the ideal beginner handgun. The revolver may not be as racy as a self-loader, but it is functional. Accuracy is very good with quality examples. The inexpensive and inoffensive .22-caliber rimfire has many advantages. Low recoil and inexpensive ammunition are the primary advantages. A good choice for beginners is the Taurus Tracker in .22 Long Rifle. This is a handgun with good grips, excellent sights, and overall quality operation. If the shooter is interested in moving to a semiautomatic carry gun, a good rimfire automatic such as the Browning Buckmark or Ruger Standard Model may be a good choice as a first handgun. Because I carry a 1911 handgun, my first choice as a rimfire trainer is the SIG 1911–22. This is a reliable self-loader with many advantages. Even if you do not choose the 1911, this is a great first handgun. While the single-action revolver isn't useful for personal defense for most of us, the Ruger Single Six .22 isn't a bad choice as a pure learning tool.

Skills build rapidly when the obstruction of heavy recoil and muzzle blast are removed from the picture. Remember—maintain a firm grip and

The author's favorite trainer is this SIG 1911-22.

The humble Ruger Single Six is a good marksmanship trainer.

use follow-through just as if you were firing a 9mm or .45, and practice will be profitable. There are good-quality .22-caliber rimfire conversion units available for centerfire handguns. The Kimber version is well made of good material. The Ciener .22 conversions have been proven in many years of use. When comparing the price of the conversion to the price of a quality .22-caliber handgun, I tend to purchase the .22 handgun. Then there are two handguns instead of a handgun and an accessory, but this is a personal choice.

A good supply of quality ammunition is a must for serious training.

Most of the quality rimfire handguns sport good sights and a good trigger. The shooter who wishes to move up in power may find a handgun with similar controls and grip shape. But a centerfire with good features will be pricier than the .22. I have said it often: a good .22 is a lifetime investment. When we are wrestling with the big bores, it is good to come back to the .22 and reaffirm our skills without the distraction of muzzle flash and recoil. While this book is concerned primarily with gunfighting skills, I am not one of those who feel that recreational shooting is wasted. Anything that adds to building marksmanship skills is good. If you have the time and funds to purchase a .22-caliber handgun as the first rung in the ladder to proficiency, you should. If you need a defensive handgun right now, then purchase a handgun that suits your current level of ability. A basic handgun-training course by a certified NRA instructor is an important step. Consider this before you begin.

GUTS, GUMPTION, AND TRAINING—TRAINING FOR PERSONAL DEFENSE

There is something that you must have if you are going to fight. If you cannot fight,

A young student is firing her first shots under the instructor's watchful eye. A good .22-caliber handgun is a great training tool.

then you will need to go somewhere and bleat like a sheep while the feral people plunder, rape, and pillage. We have too much to lose to give the bad guys the advantage. I am adept at spotting warts on society. But we cannot take them out just because we know what they are. We have to give them the first strike—*the preliminary strike*. We know that once initiative is lost, our battle is over; yet we are resigned to giving the other side all of the initiative. Sometime or other, you have to question your motivation. For most of my students, the motivation most often expressed is to survive and avoid serious bodily injury. Others feel that somehow they are in little personal danger but wish to protect their family. The questions you need to ask yourself are pretty basic: Are you able to inflict serious bodily harm upon another human being? Can you do what it takes? Just as importantly, do you have the guts to keep fighting after all appears lost?

Quite a few shooters are captured by self-delusion. They may feel smug using the .380 against a one-dimensional target that is aligned against a red berm. But when the adversary is upon us with wart hairs quivering, and the odor of tobacco, marijuana, and three days of sweat assaults our nostrils, the game is more real. I have been there. It is a gut-wrenching moment. If you hesitate, the adversary is empowered by your hesitation. You may not fear him as much as you fear making a mess of your life, but you must fight. Personal defense is sometimes messy. Life is absurd and interesting. There are quite a few people who simply cannot contemplate fighting another human being and bringing harm or drawing blood. Many of them have led a sheltered life and have never, ever had a problem that mommy and daddy did not solve for them. It isn't surprising that some of the criminal element have a similar story. They were coddled by the criminal justice system and parents who felt that it was asking too much of them to go to school and obey the rules other chil-

A good instructor, a .22-caliber handgun, and a proper frame of mind make the first shots less stressful.

dren do. They end up squandering the opportunity of America and live much as they would if born in a third-world country. Meanwhile, the child of privilege who has never had a problem cannot envision the need of personal defense. Or perhaps they see it but feel that the cops will do the deed for them.

Some of the predators have grown up in a brutal environment, with constant beatings, verbal and sexual abuse, and cultural retardation. When they look for meat or profit, they will sense weakness in the prey. They are good at sizing up a potential victim. *No*, they say, *that one would never fight back.* Often, they are correct. Some will let the feral man have the first blow or two. This is a great encouragement that often leads to a beating and death.

In the face of an attack, there are three choices. (1) Feet don't fail me now is a great idea. There is no profit in fighting. If possible, get out of Dodge! If you are in shape and a runner, run! (2) The second choice is to submit. This always results in a debacle of various proportions. (3) The third choice is to fight. Those who resist and fight live with their dignity intact the majority of the time. Over the years, I have coached

Consider this: Are you as familiar with the operation of the handgun as the cell phone? Perhaps priorities should be set in order.

many people who would fight but who could not fight well. That is a minor problem. I can get practically anyone up to speed if they are willing to fight. If you are not willing, then don't bother. Save the money spent on a gun and buy extra health and burial insurance. If you are among those who wish to carry a gun but would not use it—and there are many—get a cap gun instead. The fighting spirit must exist. If you carry a gun, get training. Otherwise you are in the position of being armed with a deadly weapon you cannot use well.

Range Work and Reality

Among the greatest impediments to training are distractions. If a student dares to bring a cell phone to a class, I will send them packing. Distractions and loss of concentration is ruinous to performance limits. I think that the best way to sum up the poor mindset many have on the range is "nothing

The T100 9mm (top) and the Stoeger Cougar 9mm (bottom) are not the most expensive handguns, but each has been proofed in an extensive firing program.

When loading on the move, always be certain the magazine is slapped into place.

The proper loading sequence is that the slide is locked to the rear and a magazine inserted.

ventured nothing gained." Quite simply they feel that nothing is really important on the range. There is no stress and no prize. We all go home in one piece, whether we perform the drills correctly or not. We have made a grand exercise of making brass and little else. Bad range habits will follow us into real life, competition, and combat. As an example, how many of you perform a weapons check before beginning your practice session? I have seen many unloaded handguns brought to bear on the range. Usually, the shooter laughs at the hollow click. Other times, shooters have forgotten to rack the slide and load the chamber of a handgun. That is not good for obvious reasons. Others have handguns with an integral-action lock, and they have locked the action and forgotten to bring the key to class. They have to borrow a gun to complete the class! Others do not bring spare magazines or enough ammo to class. Before beginning a drill, check to be certain the handgun is loaded, slap the magazine home, and ensure the safety is properly activated. Make it real just as I hope you do before venturing out from your home. My observations on the range and in training tend to qualify and isolate common range practices that would get you killed on the street.

Some students must be closely supervised simply for safety. Others must be separated from the class.

Setting up a malfunction isn't that difficult with a "snap cap" or fake round.

The Beretta 92C 9mm is accurate, but small groups are not the only criteria in combat shooting.

Here are common range problems when firing the first shots:

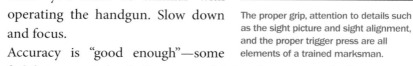

The proper grip, attention to details such as the sight picture and sight alignment, and the proper trigger press are all elements of a trained marksman.

- Going too fast—you must build skill incrementally.
- Being caught flat-footed by malfunctions—you must be familiar with operating the handgun. Slow down and focus.
- Accuracy is "good enough"—some feel that a certain level of accuracy—hitting the man-sized silhouette at seven yards—is good enough and do not strive for more. They are underachievers and probably slack in all they do. Be all you can be.

This young lady is a star student. She got up to speed quickly.

The mindset and determination are more important than anything else in the beginning.

CHAPTER SIX

CLOSE QUARTERS

GETTING HITS AT CLOSE RANGE

Getting hits at close range in a battle with a felon is the single most likely gun-fighting skill you will be called upon to execute. For those of us who have experienced such a battle, it is unforgettable. The action has been called the "Tyranny of the Moment." Your thought processes are controlled by gut-wrenching fear. A close brush with death is like a brain enema. You think much differently and more clearly afterward. If we escape death, we are pleased with the results, ideal or not.

Firing from the retention position is an important part of close-quarters battle.

Others have commented that before the event, nothing was important, and afterward, everything was important. Having observed innumerable varieties of human evil, I am aware of the endless possibility of attack. Training gives us preparation, and practice keeps us sharp. If you don't default to training, you will not rise to the occasion. When an assailant roughly the size of a tree bears down on you, weapon in hand, you may regret a lack of tactical repertoire. Mindset is important in both training and practice. I am not willing to allow a felon to usurp the prerogative of God and take my life. Some call it a protective gift of discernment; some may call it situational awareness. A "sixth sense" must be developed. Critical incidents come at you more quickly than a car wreck. Training and preparation are important but the question of why we train must be answered before we fire the first shot on the range. Facing a serial killer afflicted with acute mental decompensation can lead to an autopsy

A solid firing grip with both thumbs forward is used to control this Sphinx 9mm pistol.

Running the gun quickly and addressing multiple targets comes with skill and attention to detail.

report that is not to your liking—it may have your initials on it. That is motivation enough for most of us.

In practice sessions we should create realistic scenarios. We may stand at the seven-yard line and pour rounds into a stationary target, or we may get more realistic. Making hits at close range isn't easier than firing and hitting at long ranges. Close-range battle is more difficult when speed is added. Is the awareness of the horrific actions of our protein-fed ex-con criminal class enough to motivate us to our personal best? When facing an attacker who suffers from mild to moderate atrophy of the cerebellum as a result of drug use, your actions had best be smooth, deliberate, and immediate as a counter to violence. There is no need to practice for every specific scenario, but keep an open mind and a limber body. It isn't possible to practice for every scenario—you must be adaptive. I use past actions as a base for education. Each event is different, but every event is the same. The individual scenario may be diagrammed. In my training, I concentrate upon short-range battle, because almost all personal-defense situations take place inside

Some one-hand fire should be included in the program.

of twenty-one feet. First, understand the phases of the attack.

Every confrontation does not result in an engagement—the fight you avoid is the best one. Just the same, we should be prepared and confident.

PHASES OF AN ATTACK

1. Attack
2. Realization
3. Identification
4. Presentation
5. Acquire target
6. Engage

The attacker may be a predator. He has planned his actions and attacks accordingly. He may have been stalking the victim. He may choose to attack with stealth and will be tough to battle. The second type of attacker is known as the effective. He picks the victim on impulse or as a result of an opportunity. While he may have planned a burglary, he will rape if the opportunity is presented. He will murder to escape. His attack is often more wild and savage. The attack will come quickly. Realization that you are under attack may come with the attack, or you may realize you are going to be attacked just before it comes, reversing items one and two in my flexible table. You may see only a movement in the shoulder or in the hand, or a blur of motion. You may not see the attack. Or you may see someone firing into a crowd; it may not be a personal attack. Either way, you cannot let shock deter your response.

One of the most important skills is drawing the handgun, known as the presentation. This is the presentation from an open-front garment.

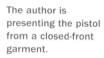

The author is presenting the pistol from a closed-front garment.

The attack triggers your presentation of the handgun from leather or from concealment. The presentation must be smooth and positive, followed by the firing stance and target acquisition. Clumsiness at close range is deadly

The hands have met in the front of the body after the presentation, and the handgun is being pressed toward the target.

to the duffer handling the pistol. Without properly executed presentation, quickly acquiring the target and staying on target is tough. There are two types of outer clothing to consider: open front and closed front. When confronted with a threat at close range, you must be able to get quickly past and around interference from clothing and complete the draw. You must practice moving clothing aside with both one hand and two hands. That's because both hands may not be available at the same time. The simplest movements may become a compound movement under stress. My experience and observations indicate that this is where most shooters fall short. To deal with threats at short range, you must master the presentation from concealed carry.

The next step is target acquisition. You cannot shove the gun in the

Firing from the retention position is vital at close range and must be practiced often.

When firing from retention, the slide must not recoil back into the body, or the pistol will malfunction.

direction of the threat and get a hit. In long-range work, the sights are aligned upon the target (long-range handgun work begins at seven yards). In short-range work—inside three yards—the handgun is superimposed over the target if the sights are not used. At intimate range, you may be shoving the pistol in the attacker's body, but you know where the bullet is going. At short range, the handgun is aimed, but the aiming sequence may not be traditional.

In this illustration, the author is firing a SIG P220 Carry .45 in the retention position.

For example, if the threat is stabbing at you with a knife, and you have the nondominant arm up to counter, the handgun will be fired from the retention position. Some skill is needed to avoid firing and striking your own body. The handgun and firing hand are locked solidly into a retention position close against the body. The slide must clear the body as it fires, the firing grip must be solid, and the firearm must be lined up with the target. This is accomplished by keeping the slide aligned with the assailant's body. At intimate-contact range, this works.

Hitting the target at close range requires practice in the appropriate skills. Many shooters are fine, deliberate shots with the handgun, but can't speed up at close range. You must be able to fire quickly and accurately. For close-range work, the best system I have found is "meat and paper." I do not teach instinctive shooting or point shooting, except in the sense that we aim at very close range with a body index as, for example, pointing the gun into a subject's abdomen at contact range. But at three to twelve feet, the meat and paper technique works. The handgun is the meat, and the paper is the threat. The slide is superimposed over the

At close range, the front sight may be superimposed over the lower part of the target for a fast hit.

At close range, a rapid sight picture will deliver excellent accuracy.

threat's body. The flats of the slide on the side must not be visible. The top of the slide should not be visible. The paper of the target surrounds the handgun's slide. This is aiming. (Do not aim for an area, but rather aim for a specific point on the target. Area aiming produces misses.) The slide is superimposed over the target with plenty of paper on each side. I repeat this, because this is an important point: the upper slide or slabs on the side should not be visible. Once you have practiced this technique and understand the principles, meat and paper works well. If you come to a range at which the handgun isn't centered in target and surrounded by target area, the sights must be used. Practice will give you a good perception of what range this is. This tactic has proven to work well in maximum-speed drills at short range.

So, it is the retention position at intimate range and meat and paper at a slightly longer range—a few feet. Next comes an extended form of shooting for ranges of ten to fifteen feet. The Applegate drill is an old one and a good

The powder gas of the cartridge adds to the effect of the bullet at contact range.

one. In this drill, the handgun is drawn as the eyes focus on and identify the target. A flash sight picture is taken as the front sight of the handgun breaks the plane between the eyes and the target. The pistol is fired, and you have a hit. This drill is fast and offers good hit potential if the shooter has practiced. This drill was usually executed with one hand, but I have found that adding the support hand doesn't limit speed and offers excellent speed for those who practice. Keep an open mind; try the Applegate a few times to see if it works for you.

Another drill that works well also involves a flash sight picture, using only the front sight. For many reasons, including a lack of lighting, the sights are not always visible. However, the front sight is usually at least partially visible. At very close range the front sight may be lifted to become silhouetted against the target. More precision is used in firing than in the meat-and-paper drill, but the bullet will strike high, because the sight is elevated. At about ten to twelve feet, aim for the belt buckle, and the bullets will strike the midsection with the front sight elevated. This is a fast but accurate technique. Practice with the personal handgun will determine the longest range at which this technique is viable.

Getting the proper stance and practicing the stance constantly will pay big dividends.

Note: More than a hundred years ago, Bat Masterson ordered his Colt with a front sight taller than standard. (That's according to Colt factory records.) A museum in the American West has a Colt Single Action Army, also with a 4¾-inch barrel and a tall, square front sight. It belonged to federal agent and gunfighter Tom Threepersons. The only conclusion that may be drawn is that these men placed great value on being able to see the front sight. I cannot agree more.

These drills cannot take the place of a well-rounded handgun-training program. You must maintain the ability to engage felons past conversational range, and you must be able to control the trigger, maintain good sight picture, and understand and execute a proper firing grip. At short range, the meat-and-paper drill is a proven lifesaver. The majority of gun battles take place at short range.

At close range, the handgun may simply be pointed—at a range of a few feet! At a longer distance, the sights must always be used.

DOUBLE TAPS AND THE HAMMER

I am going to remind you several times in these pages that defensive handguns are not very powerful compared to a battle rifle. A threat that must be
shot may need to be shot multiple times. Firing two shots at the target is
known as the double tap, although there are three distinct methods. The goal
is to stop the attack as quickly as possible; two shots increase your chances of
stopping the attack. The double tap is a multiplier of force. While any boxer
will tell you that several light blows do not equal one heavy blow for effect,
the double tap enhances the damage done by a service-grade loading. Each
individual shot that is fired is still important, and the range dictates which
tactic you will use. As an example, a hammer at ten yards would result in the
second shot missing; it would fly into the air above the threat's head. The first
technique you should master is the "controlled pair"—the technique to use if
the adversary is past conversational range. The handgun is drawn, and you
get on target. The first shot is fired as accurately as possible. As soon as the
front sight is recovered from recoil, you fire a second shot. Each shot is carefully controlled. You control your sights and recover the sight picture as soon
as possible for a third shot, if necessary, which should be delivered in a failure-to-stop drill. (See Failure to Stop Drills in Chapter 14.) If the range is
relatively short, the second shot may not be as carefully aimed as the first.
Practice can get you into the comfort zone. A quick pair at five yards, six
inches apart, is a good standard if combined with speed.

The double tap is delivered more quickly, and it's for close range. At
seven to ten feet, the double tap is controllable with practice. If you have not
practiced how to control the handgun, you will be surprised how great the
dispersal of two rounds may be at close range. The front sight is on target,
and you fire, then fire again as soon as the front sight is roughly back on
target. The shots will not be touching each other, but the effect on the target
is greater than a single hit. Close-range attacks are the deadliest, and the
double tap is best for these fights. Be certain the front sight covers the target—
or use meat and paper—and fire two shots quickly. I would carefully work
with the double tap and controlled pair at distances of three to seven yards to
gauge my own capability and determine at what range the double tap is
viable. For most of us, three to five yards is the maximum, with the controlled
pair delivering greater precision at longer ranges.

If the two shots are grouped closely or touching, you are firing too slowly. The point is to deliver two shots immediately, close together in time and each hitting the target. Two hits in six inches at your fastest speed is a reasonable goal. It is entirely possible for a handgun bullet to strike the upper torso and not penetrate to a structure important enough to stop the fight. Two bullets spaced

There are times when firing downward is a sound tactic. The bullet, if it passes through the felon's body, will quickly find the ground.

across the chest offer a much greater likelihood of an immediate cessation of hostilities.

The final double-tap technique is the hammer. It is not without controversy, but the hammer delivers two shots as quickly as possible. In this tactic, the handgun is fired as quickly as the trigger may be operated. There is only one situation in which the hammer is viable, and that is at contact range or intimate range. One scenario would be an attacker has a knife in your arm or chest as you defend and fire a hammer from the retention position. Another would be rapist has a woman about the neck, and she shoves the .38 into his body and fires twice. This is the hammer. It's a tactic worth pursuing in practice, but it isn't a viable tactic past a few feet. Contact range is the best range for the hammer.

COMBAT TRIGGER CONTROL

In the previous chapters, I mentioned the proper way to control a trigger. The first thing to learn is classic marksmanship, or you will not be able to hit the target. However, when you are practicing for close-range combat, trigger control becomes different. We cannot chase the surprise break, and indeed we should not. The smooth trigger press, waiting for the sear to break, and then waiting for a trigger reset isn't always the best program. Of course, if the shot is presented at more than fifteen yards, you slow down. The rest of the time, when performing short-range drills, the rolling trigger—or even "trigger slap," as it is called—is preferred. The trigger finger stays in motion with the trigger and never changes. A warning: When first practicing the rolling trigger, you may experience a premature discharge. You may press the trig-

At any range past conversational range, the sights must be used.

ger, come back to the first felt resistance, and press again without intending to fire. This must be avoided in practice, but control comes with meaningful practice and repetition. It is vital, I believe, that serious shooters find the pistol that suits them best—be it a first-class 1911, a Glock or SIG self-loader, or a Smith & Wesson revolver—and retain that handgun and system. Muscle memory is made up of several points, and these are contact points on the handgun. Muscle memory builds by constant practice, and the hand becoming used to the grips, trigger guard, trigger, and trigger press.

Waiting for trigger reset will slow your speed. With practice you will be able to fire quickly and ride the trigger as it resets. By the same token, taking the trigger finger off of the trigger face during speed shooting causes the firing grip to relax. Keep the trigger and the trigger finger in register, and wire the muscle memory for control; here, the trigger finger firmly presses the trigger and keeps controlling it.

CHAPTER SEVEN

THE OPEN HAND

This book is about gunfighting, but there is more to the story than handling the handgun. Part of the story is maintaining control of the handgun. This means that open-hand skills should be in place. Many years ago an instructor I respected a great deal told a class of recruits something that has never left me. He was a firearms instructor, and we also had a full load of legal classes. But he did not state his pronouncement as if it were a suggestion. It was an order. "Boys," he said, "that gun isn't there to keep you from getting your ass whipped. It is a last resort. It is there to save your life. Period."

My first chief had a strict rule in place: The handgun did not come out unless you intended to fire, not to intimidate or pull in every control situation, but when the need to fire was present. When the gun came out of the holster, the criminal elements knew that they were going to be shot if they did not immediately desist. The rest of us knew we

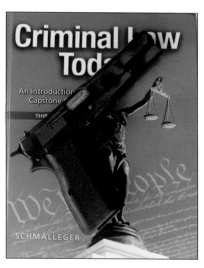

A combination of firearms skill and understanding of the law is important for everyone who carries a handgun.

The handgun is less important than the skill of the user. The bad guys do not give you a second chance.

would answer for the handgun being drawn, and the reason needed to be good.

The legal scholars pored over the continuum of force in the meantime. The instructor's vernacular, however, left a great impression, and I like to think a positive impact on his students. You absolutely must have skills in place that are less than lethal. These must include the "open hand."

THE CONTINUUM OF FORCE

More than two hundred years ago, a legal decision in a court in my home state was clear—"A BLOW DOES NOT EQUAL A SEVERE BEATING." Even though the attacker began the fight, the force that was used in turn was inappropriate.

For many years, police were simply sent on the beat with little training. Boxing, judo, karate (at least a few useful moves), and even wrestling were once taught to police officers. Arrest and control were important parts of an officer's training. Weapons carried included brass knuckles, the cosh, nightsticks, and the finest baton of all time, the Monadnock PR 24. Officers got the job done with little guidance from legal counsel—until something went badly.

Responsible trainers began to work with a force ladder that became known as the continuum-of-force doctrine—a shift from focusing on *how* to use force to *when* to use force. It has been applied primarily to the police. Other issues in the law apply to citizens, such as disparity of force.

The open hand must be available for those encounters that require less than lethal violence.

But, while the continuum of force has become a good tool for gauging actions, it is not perfect, and some feel that it isn't applicable to armed citizens or even the police in modern times. They say that the doctrine of reasonable force covers the application of force in personal defense. Still, the force continuum is useful and well worth your study.

Among continuum-of-force trainers, a doctrine emerged known as the "plus one" theory. This simply means that during an attack, you move to the next level of force, one higher than the one to which you are subjected. If the assailant pushed an officer, the officer did not simply push back, he instigated a control measure such as an arm lock. It depended upon the situation.

The following list describes the levels of threat and assault, but I changed these rules to apply to civilians. Naturally, a peace officer can't just leave the presence of a belligerent drunk; he has to control and arrest him. But a civilian should simply avoid the fight. The court may wonder why he did not.

LEVELS OF THREAT AND ASSAULT

1. **Verbal:** The courts have held that there are no such things as fighting words. The best thing to do is leave. You run the risk of being involved in mutual combat if you have a part in escalating the situation. If you frequent rough bars and engage in fights on a regular basis, you have no business wearing a gun. At this point, when someone is offended, a simple "excuse me" may work wonders. Someone bumping into you at the line to the theater isn't a reason to provoke a battle.
2. **Active resistance and assaultive resistance**: This would be interpreted in civilian terms to a shoving match. The shoving may become an assault.
3. Next come **blows, a blow to the body, or a kick**: At this point, the aforementioned open hand may be applied; a strong shove should meet the level of force exhibited in the second force continuum.
4. Finally, there is **lethal force**: While facing a knife, ball bat, or gun, your handgun must counter the assault. In fact, it would be foolish to fight back with the open hand.

Many of you have had classes in verbal judo at the corporate level. It is a good thing to understand. Often calm, clear responses, free of profanity and anger, will impress the assailant and stop the assault before it begins. Some assaults begin at the lethal level, and you must be prepared for those as well. For example, do not shove someone who has drawn a gun.

Open-hand skills begin with a shove to deter a threat.

At close range, the adversary may interfere with the presentation from concealed carry. You must have skills on hand to counter this attack.

If the revolver cylinder is grasped, the cylinder will not rotate to fire.

Give some thought to these force levels, and remember, this is a general outline for discussion, not legality set in stone. It is important to realize that an edged weapon is a deadly threat. If the assailant is standing close to you, he may close the distance and inflict death before you are able to draw, fire, and stop him. A knife never jams or runs out of ammunition.

RETENTION

In every situation, there is always at least one gun, and that is yours. When the adversary grabs for the handgun or interferes with the draw at close range, you must be prepared to counter this attack. Were you justified in drawing in the first place? When the action is close and the opponent isn't armed with a handgun, but armed with an edged weapon or blunt-impact weapon, it is reasonable to draw the handgun. If you draw without the ability to get a hit on the attacker, due to the tightness of the contact, he has the opportunity to gain control of your weapon. The handgun may be turned on you. The muzzle might cross your body, or the body of an innocent, non-involved person. If the pistol isn't gripped properly, it will be easier for the attacker to gain control of it. The weapon may even malfunction after the first shot if not held properly.

Then you have a club, and the quarters are too close to execute a clearance drill. Also, the revolver cylinder will not rotate if the adversary manages to grab it and hold it in place.

While the open-hand strike is important in these situations, it isn't all about the open hand. Footwork is important. Moving the feet, moving away from the adversary, and twisting the body away from this line of attack are important. If all falls apart, and the felon grasps the handgun, there are tactics to address the problem. The "push pull" is simple but works. When the felon attempts to pull the gun toward him, you immediately step forward and push, and step with all your strength to put him off balance. Stepping forward adds to the torque. Then pull back on the handgun. He will react by reflex, and his own movements will aid you in ripping the handgun free of his grasp.

A related subject is taking the handgun from an attacker. This isn't something to be addressed unless you are going to be shot anyway. The tactic works only if you have practiced, the assailant is close, and you are offered no other choice. Your hand shoots toward the assailants arm and then grasps the handgun. By moving quickly with the hand to a point a little behind where

Grabbing the adversary's handgun is a last-ditch tactic. You must also learn to retain your own handgun.

In this illustration, the author has grasped the slide of the pistol and is twisting upward to the side to disarm the opponent.

the handgun is, and reversing direction and following the path of the arm, you should end up with a good grasp on the pistol. As you step away from the muzzle, move it straight up using your body strength and a strong step forward. Twist and torque the gun. The pistol may fire, but with the muzzle upward, you won't be hit. The opponent's finger might still be in the trigger guard; it may be snapped, and the wrist might be broken as you torque the handgun out of his hand. Move past the assailant as you continue to twist. If the drill is properly executed, you will run away with his handgun. Never use a real firearm when you practice with another student. Fake guns, like the blue ones from Ring's Manufacturing and the red ones from ASP, Inc., are ideal for this type of work. An $8 fake Glock from a flea market works for those on a budget, but a trainer must use professional-grade dummy guns. Make certain never to begin the drill with the finger in the trigger guard. You may suffer a broken finger! And do not break the partner's wrist. Real is good, but too real is expensive.

It is less likely that the assailant will attempt to gain control of the handgun while it is holstered. This is primarily a problem for peace officers, because they carry their service weapons exposed. It is possible, however, that the assailant may discover your handgun during a scuffle. If the assailant has his hand on the holstered handgun, immediately plant your hand on his, hard, pivot on the strong-side foot, and place all of your weight on his wrist as you rip the hand upward. This is another tactic that must be practiced

Considerable force may be exerted during a grapple for the handgun; up to 100 pounds of force may be on the handgun.

The author is demonstrating the final move to disarm an opponent; the handgun has been twisted upward, and now it is coming out and down.

carefully—you do not wish to snap the sparring partner's wrist. This handgun-retention tactic works. I also recommend that anyone carrying a handgun carry a knife as backup.

The open hand, while an important tactic, simply isn't enough to retain the handgun in every scenario. If the assailant attacks from behind to gain control of the handgun, the tactic usually practiced in prison is to place one arm around the neck while the free hand grabs the handgun. This leaves the victim unconscious in short order. Thugs practice it for the obvious reason.

At short range, a draw may turn into a fight for the handgun; be prepared with proper tactics.

Trapping an arm over the larynx is the amateur's tactic. A victim who becomes short of breath also panics and puts up a terrific fight. When blood flow to the brain is limited by pressure on the artery, the subject has the feeling—and rightly so—of going to sleep. Properly executed, this is an excellent control tactic. But, if used against you, helplessness will result in a few seconds.

When under such an attack, the first impulse is to protect the handgun, but that's not possible. With one arm around the neck and the other on the handgun,

A strong strike with the hand and the retention position are important components of handgun retention.

If the adversary grabs your handgun, be prepared with a strong push-and-pull tactic to regain control of the handgun.

the assailant may also be raising you off of your feet, limiting your options. The best tactic is to draw the knife and rake it across the adversary's arm that is around the neck. Then, pivot and stab at the hand that is on your weapon. This works and results in your freedom and a seriously wounded attacker. The knife is a reasonable tool, because the assailant was attempting to gain control of a lethal weapon.

STRIKES AND PERSONAL DEFENSE—WHERE TO HIT THE OPPONENT

A strong roundhouse kick to the side of the knee works well in close-quarters combat.

The attacker is searching for a victim that goes through life asleep. Being aware and prepared will show in your stance, walk, and general composure. Avoiding trouble is always the best plan. When violence becomes unavoidable, you must be prepared to fight. A tactic that works—particularly for women—is to get loud and push back. Yell, "BACK OFF!" Do not simply accept the attack. This alerts anyone nearby that you are being attacked, and the aggressor may not wish to continue the attack if he is seen and under threat of arrest. No felon wants witnesses.

Next, you may be forced to strike the opponent. The eyes, nose, ears, neck, groin, knees, and shins are all good targets.

The attacker's stance, the slant of his body toward you, and your personal reach determine the striking point. Never rely upon skills you cannot demonstrate. A punching bag is good kit to have; practice hard. Do not strike with the fist. Strike with the edge of the hand or a forward-knuckle fist. Just under the nose, the nose, and the point of the jaw are good areas to strike. Remember, there is a line in the body that divides the best area for hand strikes and knee and foot strikes. Above the abdomen, you will strike with the hand. You may bring a knee crashing into the groin. The foot may be used to smash into a knee. Aim for a point about six inches behind the knee and thrust, and you will deliver full force. Simply aiming to land on the knee results in a miss or a blow that doesn't impart much force. Similarly, smash into the nose hard, not simply landing on the nose at the end of the fist's

A quality folding knife is a great aid in retention. The CRKT Hootenanny fills the bill.

travel. Snap the hips as you strike to deliver as much force as possible on the end of the hand. If you weigh but 110 pounds, put all of that weight on the point of your fist.

A kick to the knee is my favorite of all personal-defense tactics that stun an attacker, causing him to fall, and allowing your escape. A kick to the knee is painful. A solid kick may cause the attacker to fall. There is little chance that your foot will be caught and trapped by the attacker, while there is a good chance of the arm being trapped when you throw a punch. You do not wish to trade blows, but rather land a blow that will stop the attack and allow escape. If you can strike with your knees and elbows, you are delivering strong blows that will stun the attacker and perhaps cause his retreat.

CHAPTER EIGHT

PHYSICAL TRAINING

Over the past thirty years, I have enjoyed being trained by people who knew exactly what they were about. Perhaps some did not embrace the modern techniques, but they were ready to learn and, more importantly in some cases, ready to teach. Most of them came up from the school of hard knocks. My grandfather, Wilburn Robert Williams, had uncanny good sense and spoke of using cover and making a small target long before I learned this from professional trainers. I also grew up among the Greatest Generation, men who had seen combat and fatal errors. I listened well. In my own training classes, I have seen bright folks of all ages come to class and learn well. However, some students were so out of shape that they were unable to demonstrate tactical drills. Simply moving to cover was a major effort. They were not afflicted by disease, a bone ailment, or for the most part, age. They simply were out of shape. As I noted to my assistant, it was an embarrassment for a young person to be obese, stiff, and awkward. Simply getting them shooting safely was all I could do.

As we age, there are ailments that must be accounted for. I am no stranger to aches and pains, arthritis, and old wounds that flare up from time to time. Just a few years ago, Joyce and I climbed 780 steps to the peak of a European cathedral. Both sets of knees screamed for attention, but in tight quarters with a throng following behind us, there was no stopping! Such things are accounted for as we age, and we

Thanks to Carroll Parks for recommending the Elliptical Bike, and thanks to a SC Highway Patrolman for his gift!

modify our pursuits. Some things cannot be helped. But an inability to sprint to cover or hustle into a firing position simply because of too many cheeseburgers and donuts is inexcusable. Smoking is a killer that robs the ability to breathe and oxygenate. Today I am able to get into a firing position and take cover about as

A run around the old mill town that includes climbing steps at a brisk pace keeps the author rolling.

quickly as ever. I can compress my body behind cover, and I can sprint. I can no longer run six miles. But once I am in the position of cover, or kneeling, a well-worn and damaged knee prevents instant rising and moving. I must swing my hips, even use one hand to brace the ground and press off. When my schedule allows, I am facing corrective surgery for joint repair. Just the same, I cannot ignore physical training. And more than a quarter of the folks half my age cannot demonstrate with me. When I am no longer able to demonstrate, I will stop training others. It is embarrassing to see an instructor who can't demonstrate the tactics he is teaching.

Get out, walk, ride a bike—you will be prepared and healthy!

Swim if you can! This army guy may not wear his hat in the ocean, but then again, he may.

When hiking, carry a backpack. It's great exercise, and a little extra weight really helps the shoulder muscles.

Gunfighting is physical. Movement is important, and while the fight may not last long, practice sessions are another matter. Violent attacks are not always lethal attacks, but you still must be able to defend yourself. Violence is part of life and often a part of a free society. How you present yourself is important, and your physical training is important as well. Many shooters enjoy shooting and drills, and movement, but neglect the physical workout. Developing skill and tactics is vital, but if you do not have the physical strength and agility to execute these drills, they are worthless. Skill is important in every contest, but maintaining physical condition is as well. Those of you who hunt and have to climb tree stands, or even more challenging mountains, are well ahead of the game—or contest. By the same token, I have trained quite a few athletes. One that shall remain nameless came to the line carrying his 1911 about the slide like a football, but he progressed quickly! This is a good illustration, because you shoot as you have trained. This young man excelled on his first trip to the range. His hand-eye coordination and physical control were excellent. He wished to get up to speed on handgun skills before deploying overseas, and I like to think he did. After the training session, he and I fired at man-size targets from seven to fifty yards. He said, "Will I ever be as good as you?" As if he was an average beginner! I said, "You are the best shot with a pistol on the first day I have ever seen in my life!" Training is important, because you are disciplining

Shadow boxing works well as exercise and preparation.

both the mind and the body, and creating endurance in your body. He came to school with a trained body. His mind did the rest.

The motivation to fight off an attack is very real. An assailant will provide the motivation, as you do not wish to be killed or injured. But training requires internal, not external motivation; you are creating something where nothing existed. You should vary the exercise to destroy boredom. Walking is great, but also sprint a little to simulate sprinting for cover. Developing the leg muscles is critical. While the hands and arms are important, and most important in target shooting, the legs are your platform for

Shadow boxing keeps the body limber and builds personal-defense skills.

tactical movement. Riding a bicycle or exercise bike is excellent training; pushing yourself to full speed enhances range work and tactical proficiency. Developing a sense of balance is vital. A gradual pace to a fast tempo is a good way to train. Another discipline I find helpful is shadow boxing. It builds agility. Move with lightness, and get the arms working. Get into a fighting mindset and then begin boxing the shadow. After a while, stamina will come. You cannot be lazy and drive yourself to proficiency and fitness. You should practice until you are out of breath or genuinely tired and a little sore. Be certain of your capabilities before engaging in any type of fight or contest. Never rely upon a skill you cannot demonstrate.

CHAPTER NINE

PRESENTATION FROM CONCEALED CARRY

The presentation of the handgun from concealed carry is among the most important self-defense skills. Yet the concealed-carry draw is often overlooked or addressed in a leisurely manner. Individuals tend to repeat drills that they are good at and shun the more difficult drills. Failing to master the concealed-carry draw may result

Essential training gear includes a quality holster, such as this one from ZZZ Custom Kydex, and a good supply of spare magazines.

in a night on a cold slab with a tag on your toe. Before you begin to practice this draw, you must consider how the pistol will be carried, the position the holster is worn, and the proper support gear. A good-quality holster and gun belt must be chosen. Then the clothing is adapted to the gear, not vice versa. A compromise between fashion and tactical readiness is profitable. Tight clothing will not allow the use of a proper handgun and holster, and a dress belt will never properly support the handgun. A nonnegotiable requirement of concealed carry is a well-made, rigid gun belt made of saddle leather. Then you must decide which position to wear the handgun. The strong-side position behind the right hip is the best choice for many right-handed shooters; likewise, the left hip is the strong-side position for lefties.

The holster may be a strong-side belt scabbard, an inside-the-waistband holster, a pancake holster, or an avenger-type holster. Strong-side position is the most natural and offers a smooth, sharp draw. There should be a good reason for choosing another position for the handgun. The appendix position and the crossdraw have merit in some situations. Pocket carry is popular but limits the size of the handgun.

When choosing the holster, a service-grade design with a good balance of speed and retention should be selected. There are many cheap and generally worthless, floppy-fabric holsters to avoid. The holster and belt must be rigidly locked together so that there is no movement when you are engaged in everyday activity. The holster must be in the same position for each draw. There are good designs intended for wear under a covering garment, versus sport holsters designed for range use. Some holsters are soft for comfort but are diffi-cult to use well. Some are designed to be worn inside the pants but collapse after the handgun is

When beginning to practice the presentation, we must learn to quickly sweep away covering garments.

drawn, making it impossible to re-holster without loosening the belt and pants. A quality holster will feature a reinforced holster mouth that prevents the holster from collapsing after the handgun is drawn. The draw angle of a cheap holster is poor, because the handgun is pressed into the body. A properly designed holster will offset the handle from the body. There are acceptable compromises that allow both good concealed carry and speed.

To execute the concealed-carry draw, the covering garments are pushed aside. There are two basic types of garments, and we must practice the draw with each. These are closed-front and open-front clothing.

A closed-front garment might be a sweatshirt, while a typical jacket unbuttoned is an open-front garment. The idea of moving the garments aside is so that they do not impede the draw as the hand moves to affirm the firing grip. With an open-front garment, the hand is bladed and sweeps under the garment. This action sweeps the garment aside as the elbow shoots to the rear and the hand reaches

A closed-front garment presents special problems in executing the presentation from concealed carry.

It is fastest to raise the covering garment and draw the handgun.

It is vital that covering garments are swept away before the grip is taken on the holstered handgun.

under the handgun and scoops it from the holster. With a closed-front garment, the hand reaches under the garment, the fingers run inside the clothing, thrust the layered clothing up and over the handgun, and the draw continues. If possible, the weak-side hand lifts the garment. The crossdraw and appendix carry will be addressed later with a variation of this theme.

Meanwhile, two important things must be strictly followed.

First, don't touch the trigger until the handgun is drawn and moved to the target. The trigger finger will not be in register until we fire—not when we think we will fire, but when we have *decided* to fire. I have conducted drills beginning with the finger outside the trigger guard and with the finger on the trigger. There is no difference in speed when executing the drill in the safer, and more professional, manner.

Second, the shooter's hand must "affirm" the grip upon the first touch of the handgun. Attempting to adjust the grip after the firearm is drawn is not acceptable.

Always affirm the grip on the handgun before the draw.

Before the handgun is drawn, the grip must be affirmed.

Note that the handgun is being drawn with the grip firmly locked in place.

Instead, make sure the hand immediately closes on the handle when it reaches the handgun. That way, the grip is affirmed, and then the handgun is drawn.

I have seen students draw the handgun and then move the support hand to the firing hand and press the handgun into the proper firing position. This type of thing must be discovered and stopped immediately by a trained instructor. Such poor gun handling leads to dropping the gun, at worst, or at best, firing with an improper grip, which will result in a miss or may cause the firearm to malfunction. With the revolver, a too-high grip will result in combat heeling. The heel of the hand rides much too high. The result is a shot that goes too high. Again, the grip must be affirmed before the handgun is drawn.

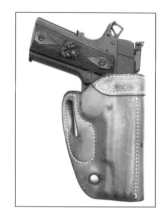

This is a well-worn Ted Blocker crossdraw, one of the best holsters in the world.

With the body bladed to the threat, the author demonstrates the proper crossdraw presentation.

The next step is bringing the handgun on target. The true presentation moves smoothly from brushing away the covering garments and drawing the handgun to coming together in the firing stance. The hands meet in front of the belt buckle, and the handgun is pushed toward the target. At close range, the handgun may move to the retention position. You may fire with one hand, depending upon the situation. Ideally the hands meet in front of the body, affirm the two-handed grip, and then push the handgun toward the target. The draw is constant, but the firing position is determined by the situation. The draw and moving into different firing positions must be practiced often for flexibility.

The primary aspects of the presentation are clearing covering garments, affirming the grip, and moving into the firing position. Many shooters do not realize that the presentation is used to move into the firing

Crossdraw is fast with practice.

All presentations from every position end with the handgun in the firing position.

position and tend to integrate the two poorly. Proper execution involves no excess movement; the shooter draws the gun and presents it to the target, aligning the sights with the eyes.

VARIATIONS

Pocket Carry

With this technique, the hand is pushed into the pocket, and the bladed hand grasps the handgun with the fingers extended. The holster is snagged on the pocket, and the handgun is drawn as the grip is affirmed. The hand must not close inside the pocket, or you will not be able to draw the handgun. The grip is affirmed as the handgun leaves the pocket. Never carry a handgun in the pocket without a holster. Lint may invade the action. The handgun may snag on pocket liners.

When drawing from the pocket, it is vital that the hand isn't closed but bladed into the gun.

Appendix Carry

The ideal appendix carry is when the support hand lifts the covering garments, and the other hand draws the gun up, out to one side, and presses it forward. Sometimes, however, the support may be busy and not accessible to help facilitate the draw.

Crossdraw

Crossdraw carry is most often done wrong. In the correct crossdraw presentation, the body is bladed to the target. The right-handed shooter will point the left shoulder at the threat, but the nondominant arm is well out of the way of the handgun's muzzle. The firing hand goes to the holstered handgun and draws the handgun straight up. The support

The appendix draw is rather simple but demands practice to master.

hand moves under the muzzle and grasps the handgun. Properly executed, the crossdraw is fast.

The primary disadvantage of conventional crossdraw is the long motion reaching across the body and then bringing the gun on target. If crossdraw is executed in this manner, the handgun is drawn across the threat's body rather than drawn into the body, reducing the accuracy of the shot and increasing the time needed to get on target.

With proper practice, the crossdraw draw is fast and effective. While specialized, it is ideal for some scenarios—a great choice for those who are seated or driving most of the day.

With the crossdraw the body is bladed to the target to address the threat.

The hand brings the handgun out of the holster . . .

. . . and into the firing position. The crossdraw is a useful draw.

CHAPTER TEN

FIRING WHILE MOVING AND HITTING MOVING TARGETS

All defensive shooters who excel must develop independence of thought. It is an unfortunate fact that I may offer hideously convincing proof of the ferocity of the criminal element. The cryptic world of death has its own mnemonic. While what we know of the criminal mind is half known and half suspected, their actions are well recorded.

If you have ever viewed a video of a police gunfight—and they are common with the widespread use of police video cameras and street surveillance—you will see that people do not stand still during gun battles. They run, duck, dash for cover, and engage in movement that is seldom tactical, but it is movement. Practicing on the static range has little correlation with such a battle. You must prepare yourself for the reality of such fluid movement. You may not be firing while moving, but you will be moving to fire. The skills developed on the range will save your life. You must understand when it is advantageous to move to a different firing position or, more importantly, move to cover.

Firing on the move is an advantage, but only at close range. Few of us can shoot accurately at long-handgun range while moving. Let's look at the training that goes into becoming proficient at tactical movement.

Move with the lower body. Most movement should be in the lower body,

In moving and firing, the author demonstrates that we must never allow our feet to cross.

When moving, the L-shaped movement is often the best plan.

below the pelvic girdle or belt line. By practicing this action, you will minimize shock transferred to the upper body. The key is to practice *rolling* movement—heel to toe. Keep the feet fairly close together and attempt to eliminate side-to-side motion. Let the knees absorb the movement. It isn't quite like gaining position to shoot the hoop in basketball, but athletes have always done well in my training classes. Practice to become smooth and fluid while going from one firing position to the other. Never cross the legs when moving.

Keeping the body rigid and tense is counterproductive. Remember the rule to keep the grip strong and independent of other movements? This is particularly true in tactical movement. The elbows are bent and ready to move into a firing position when the best position is found. This technique cannot be jerky, causing the handgun to move about; rather, it should be separated from movement—gliding, if you will. A good drill is to step out of the line of fire. Such a simple movement may be a lifesaver. Face a target and step from the line of fire, rapidly moving to the right or left, alternating movement, and then firing when you reach a point three, five, or seven yards away.

When moving, do not allow the feet to cross each other, and always be aware of obstacles in your path.

You will move, stop, and fire. Accuracy standards are not high for shooting on the move, but firing and then stopping and firing will give good results.

As you grow with experience, you will be able to fire on the move at three, five and even seven yards. A reasonable standard for a practiced shooter is to fire ten rounds covered by a six-inch circle while moving from three to five yards. A

Firing and moving are important parts of combat ability.

common shortcoming of the tactical hypochondriac is relying upon skills he cannot demonstrate. Never rely on the ability to take a shot you can't deliver. Do not attempt to make up for accuracy with ammunition capacity. Realistic firing in this type of drill will qualify exactly what your abilities may be.

As you advance in skill, move slowly and shoot at targets to the left and right, and if possible, practice pivoting and firing. Much practice in dry fire should accompany these tactical drills. The ability to deliver in this type of drill cannot be predicted by firing on stationary targets. At all times, practice trigger control. The inability to manage the trigger will never produce a miss as surely as when firing on the move. When you are

When moving, you should stop to take a shot if you are able; accuracy is enhanced.

firing on the move, the front sight is placed on the target in the center of mass. The front sight and the trigger are most important to this work. There is always a certain wobble factor, and the pistol will move, but if you have mastered the sight picture and trigger press in simple drills, you will be able to advance smoothly to firing during movement.

If you are right handed and move to the right, you will find you are able to fire well with both hands. But if you move to the left, you may be able to

When firing and moving, always retain control of the handgun; keep the arms in a shock-absorber mode and the grip firm.

Stopping, blading to the adversary, and firing is a good tactic.

use only the strong-side hand. This is simply something to be accounted for; and remember to move to the right if possible. Moving to the right, it is easier to fire to the left accurately. Take notes, and when the time comes to deliver accurate fire, know your long suits and disadvantages. You cannot know whether the adversary is skilled or not, but you may understand your own ability.

The ability to fire accurately on the move, like all handgun skills, is perishable. You will quickly lose the ability to fire accurately on the move if you have not practiced these drills. Becoming proficient doesn't mean firing a small group. If you fire small groups, then you are moving too slowly. Firing while moving will offset the skills of the adversary. Very few felons have any real marksmanship skills. But at close range, they do not need real skill to be deadly. If you are moving, you are making their target much more difficult to hit. On the other hand, you have skills that make your ability to hit the target while you are moving a more likely proposition.

A great deal of firearms training is static, and this means stagnant. Once you progress past the novice stage into the interested-student stage, you should spend less of your time firing at motionless targets. The handgun has been properly sighted in, you have learned the basics, and you need to progress. It is embarrassing to admit that we train a certain way because we have always done it this way! Traditional marksmanship training is good and has been understood for many years. Combat shooting is another matter.

Another problem is a lack of special equipment. We can pace ourselves with pretty ordinary gear as well. I have also heard students complain that they have problems hitting a stationary target. I have to ask them where they were in the class, and why they have not applied the principles they have learned. It may seem that I am critical of my students, but far from it. I have trained among the liveliest, most intelligent, and hardworking students in the world. Many are now serving in the police or military. One became the top shot in Marine Corps basic training. But I have had the other type as well. They want to be a crack shot, but they do not wish to

Advancing on the target as you fire should be practiced.

work for it. As a matter of motivation, I should mention that one of my best students was a popular local chef. He told me he wished to be able to protect his family. There is no greater motivation. He also said that when he entered the culinary industry at a fast-food restaurant, he learned everything he could, and although he worked in a humble job, he considered himself a chef. In due course, he won accolades for his work. Like the athletes I have coached, his motivation and effective mindset allow him to master anything he tackles.

The why of the equation has been answered: people move during gun battles. Now we will discuss how to train to hit moving targets. The marksmanship problem isn't severe. The gunhandling problem must be addressed. The majority of gun battles take place within twenty-one feet. Half are closer.

These steel gongs are among the finest practice targets for use when firing and moving.

Most are over in the space of a few seconds. Many of these gunfights occur in low to reduced light. This means that you will have to get a quick bead on the target, and sometimes only the front sight may be used. Tritium sights (self-luminous iron sights) are highly recommended. When fighting, adversaries will move. They may be approaching, striking your body, or getting into position to attack. Many will try to close the distance. They know their limitations, and they know that at point-blank range, they are less likely to miss. The first tactic to learn is simply stepping out of the line of fire. Move to one side or the other. To address a moving target, we concentrate on the basics of marksmanship and apply them in a dynamic manner.

I have practiced in areas that are increasingly difficult to find but that help training. A safe range with a sloping hill was one, and I rolled tires off of the hill into a ravine and practiced moving marksmanship. Later I graduated to purpose-designed rockers. IDPA and IPSC competitions are great ways to hone your skills. No, they are not combat, but combat is very individual, and these shooting contests convince you to think. Thinking ahead a second or two is an invaluable skill.

Now, to hit a moving target, use skills you have previously mastered to get the front sight on the target. No problem there. But the target is moving, and you will follow the target as it moves. The sight picture and sight alignment must be correct. The trigger press must be correct. You follow the target; don't lead the target, but stay on the center to the leading edge of the target. (No lead is necessary at the twenty feet or so of a combat engagement.) Keep the sights aligned as you press the trigger with the control you have learned in the other shooting disciplines. As the shot is fired, do not stop the handgun's movement. A jerk to stop the pistol will result in a missed shot. Keep the pistol moving with the threat, keep the front sight in the center of mass, press the trigger, and do not stop the handgun when the shot breaks. You may need a

This moving target is activated by a weight. It is a great training device.

follow-up shot, or the round may not take immediate effect. Stay on the target. Keep the handgun moving with the target as you fire, and fire again if necessary.

Many indoor ranges feature a moving-target system. This setup may only move to or away from the shooter, but it is a start. A neat trick for practicing on moving targets is to place four bull's-eye targets on a cardboard backing. Practice moving from one to the other; strike the targets in line as they are engaged. The handgun is moving, and the drill is challeng-

Firing when moving may include tactical movement and moving through doorways.

ing. The best means of practicing against a moving target is to actually fire against a moving target. By working carefully with a shooting partner, manually operated moving targets may be fabricated. I have made recommendations for use of a child's wagon as a base for movement and other improvised targets, but the following instructions are the best I have been able to provide.

First, use the standard training-target stand. Fabricate a base with two-by-six lumber. Once the stand is constructed, it is possible to purchase small wagon wheels at the hardware store. (Flea markets and yard sales often have these carts and wagons offered for a modest cost. The wheels from a rolling waste can also work.) Next, get two rolls of standard clothesline; 100-foot sections are best. Secure a line on each side. This is how your shooting partner will move the target. It is quite dangerous for anyone to stand on the range to one side or the other and pull the target stand. The answer is to place two fenceposts or other, smaller but solid posts, anything stronger than a tomato stake, in the ground at fifteen-foot intervals—a total of thirty feet apart if the range location allows this much space.

Secure the lines to the target, one on each side of the rolling target. Next, move the line from each edge of the target to the posts that you have driven into the ground. The shooting partner stands behind the shooter and

When you are firing and moving, careful attention to footwork is demanded.

operates the moving target. This is great practice. It isn't combat, but it builds confidence to hit moving targets.

Don't forget: When moving, move out of the line of fire. Move to cover. Avoid any "fatal funnel" that will draw fire, like the center of a room, the center of a door, or any place where your silhouette is outlined, offering a clear target.

CHAPTER ELEVEN

UNDERSTANDING AND USING COVER

W hen the use of cover is discussed, we must understand its nature and its importance in the scheme of things. Not being shot is at least as important and perhaps more important than hitting the adversary. Cover is anything that will stop a bullet. Conceal-ment is only that which conceals the body. As an example, a group of bushes will offer concealment and so may a sheet on a clothesline. They will not stop a bullet.

It is important to be able to fire from cover and to fire through short breaks in cover.

A good-size tree will stop practically any small-arms fire. A car door offers some cover, but it depends on the caliber and velocity of incoming fire. You need to think through these things. The first thing is to dismiss everything you have seen in the cinema. I am sure that thinking people know the difference, but after years of condi-tioning—and I enjoy the cinema as much as anyone—we will have very poor notions of reality when it comes to weapon craft.

Mattresses do not and cannot stop pistol fire. A few pistol shots cannot incite a vehicle to ignite in flames, and I am certain nothing short of a .50 BMG is capable of disabling a vehicle with a single round. Next, recognize cover. During your daily walk, be alert to possible threats, and look for poten-tial cover. When you find cover, you can place it between yourself and the assailant. This intervening mass will stop a bullet meant for you.

You must consider beforehand the decision to draw before or after you take cover. Civilians may not want adversaries to know they are armed before

The author is firing with one hand, the nondominant hand, in this exercise while using cover.

they reach cover. If you draw on the move, the draw and movement will conflict with one another. If you are going to fire as you run for cover, there should be a realistic expectation of striking the assailant. A zigzag sprint to cover is never a bad idea. Once you reach cover, do not become married to it. If you are able to move to a more advantageous position, do so. The goal is not simply to keep from being shot, but to escape, with shooting the adversary less of a concern. When you move to another spot of cover, use the L-shaped run—a long leg and then a short leg. Or run a short leg and a long leg—whichever is best. If you stay at the spot you entered cover, you are more vulnerable to being flanked. If you are behind cover, and the adversary is advancing with fire, you should move as far as possible from the initial contact point. If you are behind a wall, this is possible, but not if you are behind a pole. Let the adversary wonder about your exact location.

Once you have found cover, maximize it. You should compress or even contort your body behind modest cover. A utility pole, for example, stops bullets, but the width isn't ideal; your elbows will be exposed unless you align yourself perpendicular to the cover. While this is better than nothing, the adversary need only flank the utility pole to be in a position to fire with good effect. Hopefully you will be able to neutralize the threat before he does so.

The author is demonstrating firing from cover with a good offset between the cover and his firing position.

While making yourself a small target, also avoid plastering your body against cover. When you do this, you severely limit tactical movement, yet hugging cover is a basic instinct. If you are too close to cover, a bullet striking the object, or the edge of the object, may strike your body. As an example, if you take cover behind a vehicle, the offset of your body should measure several feet. A bullet striking the vehicle may bounce into your body. You will be better shielded from observation if you are a few feet back from cover, but your cover will be just as good. If the adversary attempts to outflank you, the chances are he will expect you to be plastered against the vehicle. If you are hard against cover, you will not have an advantage.

If you must fire from behind a vehicle, you will be much more visible firing over the vehicle as you break its silhouette. By emerging quickly from cover a few feet back, out of symmetry with the vehicle, you become a much more difficult target. When you fire from cover, do not shoot over the top of cover, but fire from one side of cover. Your tactical position is much better.

If you crowd cover and lead with the handgun, you just may have the gun grabbed by an adversary!

Also be aware that if you are close to cover while shooting, a spent case may strike a wall and actually bounce back into the gun's ejection port, causing it to jam. This has happened on occasion in competition and requires some skill to quickly clear the problem. Be aware of this possibility;

When taking cover, do not plaster yourself against cover; this shooter is too close to cover.

This isn't the ideal cover location; too much of the body is exposed.

The author practices firing from around common cover, a vehicle. The steel wheel provides excellent cover.

Firing from behind cover, the author has the gongs rolling from .45-caliber hits with the Smith & Wesson Model 25.

This is a good position for firing from behind cover, with good offset.

to understand it, shoot from the barricade and notice how cartridge cases bounce from the structure, across your line of sight, and into your body.

Vehicles are common cover, but car doors are not proof against incoming fire. A 9mm Luger +P or .357 SIG will penetrate two car doors in line, unless the bullet is stopped by internal bracing or the window regulator mechanism. The rear quarter panel of a vehicle is thin. The forward section of the vehicle that houses the engine will stop all common small-arms fire. (When a load is labeled "Penetrator" this applies to humans, not steel. The most powerful .357 Magnum revolver or .308 rifle will make only a lead splash on an engine block.) The radiator and soft parts are easily perforated, but this isn't a concern if the engine block is used for cover. Vehicle steel wheels are excellent cover, especially in tandem with the forward-engine section. Shooting at vehicle glass is another matter.

Windshields are hard on bullets. Incoming bullets usually strike low in relation to the point of aim. A bullet fired from inside the vehicle through glass strikes high at the seven-yard line. Side glass shatters on impact. If you have to shoot into a vehicle, which is unlikely but possible, the side glass is the best option. Common handgun cartridges are severely degraded in performance by windshield glass. If you are forced to fire from inside the vehicle at an assailant, aim at least several inches low at three to ten feet. The bullet trajectory will be moved upward by the glass. You should explore and develop a working idea of cover for your advantage and also

Firing standing allows the shooter to move quickly. The barrels represent cover.

understand what type of cover your adversary may take.

In the home, pistol bullets can pierce Sheetrock and common doors. However, brick walls stop slugs, as does heavy wood bracing.

Be aware that bullets may bounce. Modern high-velocity, hollow-point handgun bullets will most often flatten against hard objects. Bad guys do not usually use jacketed-hollow-point bullets, but whatever they can steal or find. Even if you are

It isn't the best program to step out of cover and expose yourself, as illustrated.

Far better to take a position to one side and avoid a fatal funnel outlining your position.

You cannot always choose your cover; a good firing position is the one that works!

A few shots into masonry confirm that just anything isn't cover!

close to a bullet striking a wall, fragments are dangerous. Any bullet may bounce up from a concrete surface. For example, a bullet fired under a vehicle may well bounce along the ground until it stops. It isn't difficult to destabilize a bullet. The bullet will usually, but not always, stay close to the ground after a ricochet, depending upon the angle. Cover, however strong or weak, is a great advantage. You should practice taking cover when running your firing drills. Develop a realistic expectation of your ability to move to cover and shoot from it.

CHAPTER TWELVE

HOSTAGE RESCUE AND FIRING IN CROWDS

I t isn't unusual for felons to take a hostage. Many small town punks are charged with kidnapping. I once charged such a moron with kidnapping his girlfriend. (His drug use had aggravated what it was meant to allevi-ate.) He reacted with, "But I didn't ask no ransom; that ain't kidnapping!" Taking a hostage against that person's will is a serious offense.

At first, this seems like a good group, but good enough just isn't good enough. The range was fifteen yards, long range for a hostage-rescue shot. In an actual incident, one shot is all you have.

Hostages are taken daily in this country; two such cases made the news this month in my home county. On another occasion, a man held a knife to his wife's throat and ordered the responding officers to drop their guns. The proper course would have been to retreat, negotiate, or refuse. They put down their guns. The man charged them and severely stabbed both officers. He escaped, and one of the officers nearly died. As detailed in the Joseph Wambaugh book, *The Onion Field*, even cops are taken hostage. Do not ever give up your gun. You have signed your death warrant when you do so. The hostage will probably die as well. When the bad guy gives up his gun and surrenders, he goes to prison. If you give your gun up, you are dead.

When soldiers are forced into a law-enforcement role, and peace offic-ers are forced to engage in military-type operations, confusion occurs and concern is evident. During the past few decades, many have expressed concern over the militarism of police forces. By the same token, unrealistic restraints and limiting rules of engagement have resulted in needless casual-ties among our servicemen fighting in Iraq and Afghanistan. Part of the

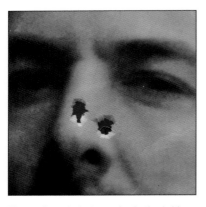

The preferred aiming point is the bridge of the nose.

rationale behind this chapter is to provoke debate and response. I do not have all of the answers. But I have no illusions concerning the adversaries we face.

The perversity, depravity, and viciousness of our enemies overseas are unprecedented in modern warfare. Much the same may be said of the criminal element in the United States. Terrorism, by definition, is the use of violence to bring about political change. But our enemy does not wish to achieve a political end. He wishes the destruction of both America and Israel. Still, "terrorist" is a fitting description, and its negative connotations are suitable. What is our outlook? Many of our public buildings (including auditoriums, schools, and churches) are open as a sieve. There is sometimes a restriction of access to a single point. These checkpoints are the obvious frontline of defense, but the security officers at these points are unarmed. It is at these points that a terror attack may be stopped by immediate action.

It is important to note that immediate-action drills are of the same type used to interdict an active shooter. American peace officers, like American soldiers, are recognized as the best in the world. But they have a clear problem—their training is the best, but is it relevant to the present situation? American cops are trained to take violent offenders alive when possible. We hold offenders at gunpoint and give them a chance to live. The degree of difference

Rachel demonstrates firing an FNH .45 at a slightly downward angle.

between allowing a bank robber to escape and allowing a terrorist to escape is a great measure. Terrorists must be shot and killed immediately upon identification. Attempting to take gun-wielding terrorists into custody can be fatal for the officer or civilian. Terrorists seldom work alone. And how do you arrest a suicide bomber? A reluctance to use deadly force is seen as a weakness that terrorists will exploit. A terrorist is not a criminal. He is an enemy of the republic. He may be a U.S. citizen, as Islamic terrorists are actively recruiting in America, particularly in our prisons. Potential terrorists exist in the ranks of our protein-fed, ex-con criminal class. Already, gang members in Chicago have accepted money to promote terrorist acts. The FBI thwarted that event years before 9/11.

It is simply not possible or tactically sound to issue any type of warning when confronted with a terrorist. The only response must be immediate, lethal force. The officer on the spot must have his tactics down solid and his head on straight.

> *There is but one answer to be made to the dynamite bomb, and that can best be made by the Winchester rifle.*
> —Theodore Roosevelt on Anarchists

> *The main difficulty is to fire accurately when your first impulse is to bring everything you have to bear immediately.*
> —Benjamin Netanyahu

What is the likelihood of such an event? Increasingly, the likelihood isn't great, but the plausibility is. Far more common is the bad guy who takes a helpless child or woman hostage. I have dealt with a few. There were no deaths involved. Just the same, mine were unarmed or armed with blunt weapons. When they are armed, there is little chance of the situation ending well. Few, if any, of us are as well trained as the FBI tactical team that in 2013 rescued 16-year-old Hannah Anderson from an armed kidnapper in Idaho. He fired at the rescuers while in close proximity to the girl, but the FBI hit him five times. Seldom is the victim held to the subject's body; often they are moving or driving in a vehicle. A few years ago a pair of felons from Greenville, South

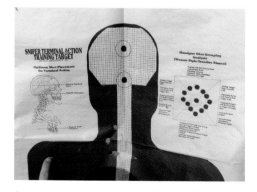

As you can see, only a narrow band of the body offers an immediate shutdown if struck with a bullet.

The author is shielding the pretty girl.

Carolina kidnapped a woman and fled to Florida. The Florida Highway Patrol stopped them and killed one by firing through the windshield. The victim was unhurt. Also in 2013, Sergeant Jeff Young of the Bannock County (Idaho) Sheriff's Office was covering a hostage taker. When the man moved his pistol to the head of the hostage, an eighteen-year-old boy, Young took the shot at seventeen yards and ended the standoff.

Unfortunately, the cases do not always end well. In another incident, a felon held a woman at gunpoint. As the police approached, the perp shot at them. Gunfire was returned, and the hostage died. In another case, a burglar was firing wildly, and shots were exchanged. A child died. Any type of shooting is a grim business. You must have absolutely mastered the shot to attempt this type of shooting. I am including this chapter as much as a warning not to attempt the shot as offering the reason why you should learn the shot. This isn't a contradiction—never rely upon a skill you cannot demonstrate. Practice the shot. If the adversary is close to the victim, the best course is to retreat and take cover. If you are able to take the shot on the bridge of the nose, do so. Otherwise, don't take the shot if the skill and composure aren't there.

FIRING IN CROWDS

We are not firing at crowds or into crowds, but rather firing while surrounded by people. Not long ago in my hometown, a gunfight between two factions erupted with almost two dozen shots fired in a mall—without a single person stuck by a bullet.

An incident that occurred when I was a child left an impression on me that I understand far better today—that a person without tactical training, but possessed of good sense, can handle many dangerous situations. At a county fair, a large, belligerent drunkard had knocked about several people.

While a viable tactic, firing upward cannot be practiced live fire at the range.

The offset from cover exhibited in this drill limits visibility while maximizing cover.

An armed security guard arrived and was immediately cold cocked. As the guard lay on the ground, the drunk knelt on one knee and fumbled with the guard's handgun in its holster. Remember, there is always one gun on the scene, yours, and it may be turned against you. The man stood up with the gun in hand. An older gentleman in overalls went to his knees very close to the man, drawing his own revolver. I am certain the handgun was an old top-break .38 Smith & Wesson. Five shots rang out. The drunkard staggered, dropped the guard's gun, and collapsed. The old man knelt and fired upward to avoid any danger to the crowd.

When the handgun is fired, the barrel is seldom perpendicular to the earth, but pointed slightly downward or slightly upward, depending upon the range involved. The handgun's geometry and the manner in which the sights are presented to the eyes mean that the bullet will usually find its way to earth in less than 100 yards. Just the same, we realize that the problem of a bullet carrying far past the area of the shooting event is a real concern. Most gunfights occur at relatively short range. If the individual must fire to stop death and mayhem, then crouching and firing upward into the heavy bone structure of the adversary is a tactic worth considering. Take care to aim for a lower spot than you usually do. The bullet is angling upward. A shot fired in the normal manner would simply rake across the flesh and not produce a wound with the potential to stop the assailant. Aim several inches below the heart, as an example, in order for a raking wound to take effect.

When caught in an active-shooter situation, or even a robbery in a crowded store, the first thought should be for personal safety rather than stopping the bad guy. If he robs and runs, that is good; the police can arrest

The author isn't emerging in the middle of the doorway, but avoiding the fatal-funnel effect by staying to one side.

him later under conditions they control. But he has control at the moment of his choosing during the attack or robbery. If you must fire, do so without hesitation. I have seen individuals practice drills that, for want of a better description, I call "Secret Service drills." There is no organization better trained and more respected than the Secret Service, whose agents are willing to take a bullet for the president. A tactic in such a situation might be to move in front of your spouse or children. You are not alone all of the time, are you? How much of your time involves family members? Better consider their place in the battles—one more reason to avoid the battle when possible. Running in front of your family to shield against bullets is a viable tactic if the loved ones are the targets. But if not, and you run in front of them and draw fire, you and your family are now a beacon for attack. While I have practiced this tactic, I have also practiced others.

I think particularly in the study of active-shooter events, a good tactic is to draw and fire and even run at the shooter, which could cause him to stop firing at anyone but you. He will address the threat. You will either draw fire away from your family, or you will stop him. As a note on active shooters, I never recommend firing without the greatest possibility of a hit. However, on several occasions involving criminals and the psychotic class of shooter—and terrorists as well—the first sign of incoming fire prompted them to stop and kill themselves. That isn't a bad outcome. Be aware of this possibility in a true active-shooter situation. Unlike conventional shootouts, it seems that even a round into cover that surrounds the active shooter may precipitate his demise, by his own hand. Nothing may be taken as gospel, but it seems a good bet in a desperate situation with no good answers. The worst answer is to do nothing.

I usually recommend service-grade ammunition for all occasions, loads with a balance of expansion and penetration. Those engaged in church security or working in tight quarters might consider the HPR Ammunition's Black Ops load. This is among a very few, specialty pistol loads designed to fragment and offer low ricochet potential. This ammo is also reliable and accurate enough for any conceivable duty. In every situation, only marksmanship will carry the day. When confronting a hostage situation, the shot must immediately neutralize the

HPR's rapidly fragmenting Black Ops load is worth considering for some scenarios. Unlike some frangibles, this load is quite accurate.

assailant. When firing in crowds, there is no room for error.

Often we are forced into areas in which we have no expertise or training. As an example, there is no good reason to clear a house if there is no family member in the home who is in immediate danger. I am certain we have all seen the room-clearing exercises on popular TV dramas and perhaps police videos. We have also seen events at Columbine and other school shootings, to name but a few, in which the police surround a building with their guns pointed and wait. Then after the shooter is done killing people, they count the bodies. I find this morally bankrupt. But this is a typical official response. The usual room-clearing drills are for those situations in which there is no threat expected. A threat behind cover would make short work of such an entry. A dynamic entry, complete with flash-bang devices, is the answer for a real threat. I am not equipped for a dynamic entry, and you probably are not, either. Speed, aggression, and determination combine for a true dynamic entry.

In our own home, we may go through the door and find an adversary waiting. We may rise out of bed to investigate the animal that has knocked over the trash and find a human adversary. It happens. Many pages have been spent in describing the fatal funnel or the target indicators that must be avoided. In short, do not present yourself in the doorway which could silhouette you in the light or the door frame, making you a target. I think that it would behoove us all to go over our domiciles and consider where an invader may hide.

For example, my modest living room offers no sanctuary at all. The old mill house is quite charming in its brevity; the sectional sofa is pressed against the wall, and the recliner is against a bookcase. The hall, however, is another matter. At the end of the hall, there is the possibility of a quick duck into the guest bathroom, the master bedroom, or the dining room. Perhaps someone could stand on the tall steps leading to the garret. That is where things could get hairy. I might be better served to retreat, sprint to the back door, and enter there; I'd find myself in a much better situation. So, canvass your own home, and do a similar evaluation.

The fatal funnel may apply in any situation, in the home or office, or even when behind cover. Understand this and train accordingly. For example, standing in the middle of the sidewalk makes you an easy target. But sidestepping to one side will cause your body to blend into the building and make you a more difficult target. If you are not going into the area to rescue a screaming child or your spouse—and I think that all of us would go headlong to save loved ones, even if armed with only tooth and nail—then exercise all caution. Do not ignore the possibility of multiple threats. Hostage rescue will sometimes mean entry into a dangerous space. You are on your own with no backup and only your skills to save you. Keep your eyes open and your mind working. Strenuousness in practice pays big dividends.

CHAPTER THIRTEEN

MALFUNCTION DRILLS

Handguns are devices of irreducible complexity. One part fails, and the machine stops working. Thankfully, breakage is rare. Quality firearms tend to wear in a controlled and even manner. A lack of cleaning and lubrication promotes eccentric wear. Once such wear begins, it progresses rapidly. Handgun maintenance is essential. Regular cleaning and proper lubrica-

Malfunctions occur with any machine, but most often with junk guns.

tion is important. But malfunctions may occur with the best-maintained handgun. The problem may be shooter related, ammunition related, or a magazine issue. True jams are rare, but stoppages are not. There are different types of malfunctions, and you must be able to clear them. Staring at the handgun and shaking it will accomplish nothing.

Let's look at clearing common malfunctions of the self-loading handgun.

FAILURE TO FIRE, OR TYPE-ONE MALFUNCTION

The hammer falls or the striker strikes the cartridge, but the pistol does not fire. The magazine may not be seated correctly, or it may have loosened from the magazine catch, and a cartridge failed to feed. The cartridge may be defective. Here is the clearance drill.

The handgun remains in the firing position. The trigger finger is alongside the frame. Tap the magazine to be certain it is seated. Next, grasp the rear of the slide and rack the slide to the rear, simultaneously turning the handgun at a 90-degree angle so that the cartridge in the chamber is ejected

The cartridge case in the ejection port is the dreaded stovepipe jam.

To clear a stoppage, first tap the magazine to be certain it is seated.

Next, grasp the rear of the slide to clear the ejection port.

The pistol is now cleared.

The pistol is now ready to fire—Tap, Rack, Bang!

and falls to the ground. Let the slide snap forward. Never maintain control of the slide when loading; always let it snap forward. Otherwise you may experience a "short cycle." A cartridge is heavier and longer than a spent case and needs more help clearing the ejection port. Now aim at the target and press the trigger. The handgun should fire. This drill is called, "TAP, RACK, BANG."

While executing this drill on the range, do not always fire, then alternate firing and not firing. Always be in control. There is a chance you will suffer a malfunction and not be justified in firing that shot after you have cleared the dud cartridge or loaded the chamber. This is an easy drill to practice. You may use the dummy cartridges offered by several makers and available from Brownells.com.

TYPE-TWO MALFUNCTION: FAILURE-TO-EJECT DRILL

The handgun doesn't fire. The slide is not locked forward. Cant the muzzle up and scan for a cartridge case in the ejection-port stoppage. Tap the magazine. Whether you have a cartridge case in the port or not, rack the slide, and be certain that the brass caught in the ejection port is ejected. To practice this drill, simply insert a spent case between the breechface and barrel.

TYPE THREE MALFUNCTION: A FEEDWAY STOPPAGE

A cartridge is in the chamber, and another cartridge has attempted to load and is butted into the chambered cartridge. A spent case may not have been extracted, and the following cartridge case has rammed into the spent case. This malfunction is often described as the most difficult to clear, but with practice, it can be cleared quickly.

With this drill, you remove the magazine and lock the slide to the rear. Sometimes there will be a round in the chamber, and the round attempting to feed from the

This happened during a gun test; a case is in the chamber, and a fresh round is running up.

magazine may be hard against it. The cartridge in the chamber may be live, or it may be a cartridge case that did not eject. The magazine may be stuck to an extent, and you must forcefully rip it from the pistol. A cartridge in the feedway will be cleared when the magazine is removed. Let the slide snap forward three times. This will ensure the cartridge or case in the chamber is clear. Lock the slide to the rear. Now load a fresh magazine. Let the slide run forward to chamber a fresh cartridge. This is a difficult problem to simulate with dummy cartridges, but it can be done. Lock the slide to the rear, and

Forcefully seating the magazine is a requirement for good function.

insert a dummy round in the chamber. Load the magazine with a dummy round, insert the magazine, and let the slide run forward. You have now set up a type-three malfunction.

Most of the steps of these drills are the same as they begin, but the individual malfunction demands specific remedies.

REVOLVER MALFUNCTIONS

Typically, if a revolver stops working, it is out of the fight. However, there are a couple of problems that may be fixed on the spot. If the revolver's cylinder will not open, the ejector rod may have become loose. This isn't supposed to happen with modern revolvers. New rods are

The revolver cartridge has stayed in the chamber or slipped under the ejector star; this can be difficult to clear.

now designed to tighten under recoil, not loosen, but it happens. The cure is to carefully hold the hammer to the rear just enough for the bolt stop to drop and allow the cylinder to be turned in the opposite direction of normal rotation. This will usually tighten the ejector rod enough to open the cylinder.

The ejector rod of a revolver sometimes becomes bent and may also loosen.

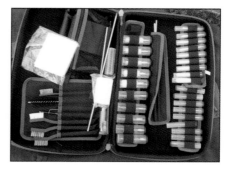

A good-quality cleaning kit is a must for the serious handgunner.

The cylinder is also involved in another problem. If the muzzle is not pointed straight up when the spent cartridge cases are ejected from the cylinder, a spent case may become stuck under the ejector star. The only answer for this one is to point the muzzle up, use the support hand to keep the ejector star open, and pick the cartridge case out with the tip of a knife or whatever is available. Be certain when unloading the revolver to always keep its muzzle up to eject spent cartridge cases.

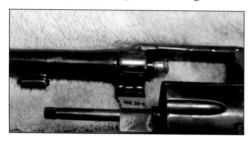

This revolver has suffered a bullet stuck in the forcing cone; there is no quick cure. It was driven out with a wire rod.

A minimal cleaning kit goes a long way toward handgun reliability.

Malfunctions in a gunfight are survivable, but only if you are prepared. Preventive maintenance—routinely checking the magazines, magazine springs, recoil springs, and keeping the pistol clean and lubricated—is important. Quality ammunition of proven reliability is a must; so is using the proper grip to give the slide a stable platform to recoil against.

When ejecting spent cartridges from a revolver, be certain the muzzle is pointed upward and give the ejector rod a good push to avoid malfunctions.

CHAPTER FOURTEEN

FAILURE-TO-STOP DRILLS

A comprehensive training program must include drills for worst-case scenarios. Our skills are not in place to deal with the average day. We are training for the worst case. It is never enough to train to be just good enough to pass the state qualification or department trial. "Failure-to-stop" drills are designed to deal with an attacker who has been shot, but he keeps fighting. Failure-to-stop drills may be termed a backup drill when all else fails. This drill is executed after the initial hits fail. When you consider the power available in a handgun, the likelihood you will need multiple hits to stop an assailant is very real. Compared to the .223-caliber rifle or 12-gauge

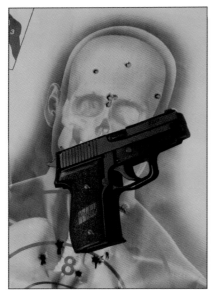

With one group fired at a long twenty-five yards and the other at seven yards, the SIG P228 is accurate enough for a failure-to-stop shot.

Left to right, 9mm, .40, .45, .223, .308, and 12-gauge. The pistol calibers have only a portion of the energy of the rifle and shotgun. They must be used as efficiently as possible.

shotgun, the "weak .38" and "strong .45" are more alike than different. Calibers beginning with a four—the .40 Smith & Wesson, .44 Special, .45 ACP, and the similarly powerful 10mm—are more likely to stop an assailant with a minimum of shots, but they are not infallible.

Many street drugs are based on pharmaceutical drugs that were designed as painkillers, which can keep a dope-addled attacker in the fight. Only actual damage will stop an attack. A human being is about the size of a deer and about as hard to put down. Humans are susceptible to shock, while the animal does not know it has been shot, but the correlation is relevant. Once the first

Once the ball goes up, only accurate fire will stop an assailant.

shot has struck, but hasn't stopped the attack, subsequent shots may not prove immediately effective. A shot delivered to the arterial region with a cartridge of sufficient power—beginning with the 9mm +P—is likely to cause a shutdown, but all shots are not well placed in a gun battle. We must be ready for immediate action to stop the threat.

The best course is always to make the first shot count. Nothing I can say about failure-to-stop drills is intended to take the place of an accurate first shot. But it isn't always this easy. When the attacker does not react to shots, there are several points to consider. First, you may have missed the target. Second, the hits may not have taken effect. Third, the target may be wearing a bulletproof vest. If the initial application of marksmanship has failed, then you may not be up to properly executing a failure-to-stop drill, as even greater precision is demanded. Practice until this problem is eliminated.

What if the adversary is wearing a bulletproof vest? This plate will stop even a .308 rifle bullet.

This target has been center punched, hit in the pelvic region, and suffered a headshot during training.

When the hits have not taken effect, move your point of aim to a different part of the body. The legs are never a good target; they are relatively small, moving, and hitting them does not necessarily result in a stop. Even if the opponent's femur is broken, and he falls, he may still be able to return fire, and he may be a smaller target on the ground.

Instead, change the point of aim to the pelvic girdle. There are many blood vessels and also a heavy bone structure in this area. A bulletproof vest that is worn under normal clothing seldom covers this area, because it would interfere with movement. A military-type, lower armor plate would be obvious. Fire for the belt buckle or slightly to one side and below. The complex circulatory system will be damaged, and blood loss should result in a rapid shutdown. There is some evidence that shots to the lower body cause the most painful of all wounds.

Pain cannot be counted on to stop a bad guy, but highly experienced fighters as diverse as Border Patrolman Bill Jordan and guerilla-leader Mao Tse Tung have commented on the effectiveness of the abdominal shot.

This shooter has hit the center, switched to the lower quadrant, and finally taken a headshot.

Firing from cover, and firing accurately, is the best answer to a failure to stop.

The second variation of the drill is more difficult. This requires firing for the cranial region. A head shot is possible, because the range is usually short and also because the head will be stabilized if the attacker is aiming at you. This drill demands attention to every component of marksmanship. Once the initial shots have failed to take effect, you cannot hesitate and assess the situation, but you must immediately transition to the failure-to-stop drill. With an adrenaline dump and other effects upon the body, you must fire accurately to stop the attack. The drill means a shot to the head and, properly, the bridge of the nose. I have in my files an account of a 110-grain .38 Special JHP bullet that struck a felon squarely on the occipital ridge. He fell and ceased all movement, so the shot was successful. However, as the ambulance arrived, he sat up and complained of a terrible headache. The bullet had flattened on his skull, to perhaps one inch in diameter, without penetration. On another occasion, a 230-grain FMJ bullet from a .45-caliber pistol struck a hostage taker in the side of the head. The bullet traveled under the scalp, rode the curve of the skull, and exited the rear of the scalp. The felon turned from

The primary objective in personal defense with a handgun is accurate fire. Where that fire is delivered means the most, and we must be prepared for the most difficult shot.

These students are learning to deliver accuracy at the prestigious Gunsite Academy.

If possible, get behind cover and deliver accurate fire until the adversary is stopped.

the hostage to an officer, but a second shot, delivered to the eye socket, was true. The lower jaw has also proven resistant to bullets. If the cranial shot is not delivered properly, it may fail.

A combination of a shooting-and-moving assailant will add to the difficulty of executing this drill. If you have not practiced your skills, a failure to stop on a motivated felon will result in you being shot or killed. Failure-to-stop drills are among the most difficult tactical drills and must be mastered as part of the tactical arsenal. The proper course of action is to make the first shot count the most. An equally proper course of action is to be prepared for the shot to take no effect at all. When this happens, the failure-to-stop drill is executed.

CHAPTER FIFTEEN

SPEED LOADS

Positive manipulation of the magazine release with one hand is demanded when learning speed loads.

The shooter has punched the magazine release and ejected the empty magazine.

I t is important to learn to quickly replenish ammunition. The first hurdle is to convince the shooter to carry a spare supply. With the self-loader, it isn't difficult. When carrying concealed, I routinely use a Wright Leather Works magazine carrier. Flat and unobtrusive, this device is carried on the weak side.

When the subject of speed loads comes up, the argument against learning them is that training time is at a premium. If speed loads are not often used in combat, why should we take time to learn them? The same may hold true for many disciplines, and we have to continue to address each with the time needed to gain proficiency.

This Wright Leatherworks magazine carrier is ideal for most uses.

A few years ago, I was asked to work up a speed-loading regimen for the semiautomatic shotgun. The agency in question issued semiauto handguns and was transitioning from pump-action shotguns to semiauto shotguns. That's because some officers using semiauto pistols and carbines were forgetting to pump their shotguns after each shot! They cocked the piece initially, fired, and then tried to press the trigger again to fire without manually cocking the shotgun. Consequently, the semiautomatic shotguns were evaluated and issued. There are important differences in the manually operated shotgun and the pump in reloading, and we were successful in working up a technique well suited to the semiauto shotgun. This research gave me pause for introspection.

Many times over the years, I have trained people with handguns or long guns that were far from my first choices, but which served the individual or agency well. Seldom if ever has training been leisurely. I have not always been able to impart shooting techniques as thoroughly as I would have liked in the time frame allowed. I have concentrated upon marksmanship. The stance, grip, firing points, sight alignment, sight picture, and trigger compression are most important.

But with time at a premium for all of us, is mastering the reload important? And if we carry spare ammunition—and quite a few off-duty officers and civilian shooters do not—how much ammunition should we carry? The issue is important enough that several otherwise-good weapons systems have been discarded simply because of the difficulty in replenishing the ammunition supply. The Garand rifle and the Magnum revolver are examples. Let's look at the issue from as many perspectives as possible.

The soldier on patrol carries as much ammunition as he can. Like the cowboy on the range or the border patrolman on duty in the vast west, he must rely on what he can carry. Food and ammunition may be replenished by air support, or they may not. Extra ammunition may be shared with our friends, and if the GI has the need to swim or climb, he may discard part of his load. Soldiers, God bless them, are a different breed.

Most of us are interested in carrying spare ammunition on and off duty. If I had not been a peace officer, I would have lived a dull life. All of my difficulties came while in service. I had no need to reload and carried only the rounds in the handgun when the ball went up. I became overexcited exactly once, when a slithering reptile made a move for me. I fired six .357 Magnum cartridges as quickly as I could, and he was finally impressed. A solid hit caught him in the coils, and he landed like a pretzel in the grass alongside the highway. While he was a big snake, he was a small target. Had I hit the copperhead the first time, I wouldn't have needed shot four, five, or six, whichever did the business. During a barricaded-gunman incident, a friend stuck his 9mm in a house window and emptied the pistol, destroying a Frigidaire. During a standoff, another friend fired 35 rounds of .38 Special from a box of ammunition he kept in the cruiser. Whether the rounds were needed is debatable, but they were fired.

Other incidents, including a sniper in a high-rise apartment and an armed standoff in a home, demanded copious amounts of ammunition, few of which hit targets. Whether cops need that much ammunition, we still like to have it. But in none of the cases involving a high-round count was the ammunition dispensed from a belt carrier. The extra ammunition, both shotgun and handgun, was carried in the cruiser.

My circle of friends—and I have many who have been in quite a few total shootings and investigated many more—cannot remember a single instance of a reload from the belt during an action. Still, there are good reasons for carrying spare ammunition. We may fall into the proverbial deep end of the creek.

Border Patrolman Bill Jordan knew most cop gunfights are short-range affairs, taking place at a few feet and finished in a few seconds. But he also gave the example of the man who drowned in a creek of average three-foot depth. That critical example is one worth preparing for.

In Jordan's day, some practice went into reloading the revolver, but not much about speed loading. We leisurely reloaded the revolver between firing strings, and it was pretty much the same with the semiauto. No one gets in a hurry between drills. Range work should build complete familiarity with the handgun, and loading, unloading, and manipulating the controls should be second nature.

There is a difference in the mindset of those carrying revolvers and semiautos, and it is

This is the fastest of all revolvers to reload, the Colt 1917 with .45 ACP full-moon clips. Most of us will choose a lighter revolver for carry, but this is a viable home-defense system with modern versions.

reflected in the amount of ammunition we carry when deploying either. The revolver man realizes that the shots in the piece are what is important, not the reloads on the belt. These are the rounds that count. If he needs to reload and hasn't got the business done, something is awfully wrong. The defensive handgunner often drops the five-shot .38 into his pocket and doesn't carry spare ammunition. He is more likely to carry a spare gun than a speedloader device for revolvers. Relying on the backup gun is a technique called the "New York Reload"—much faster than a speedloader!

The fellow packing a semiautomatic will appreciate the firepower, be it an eight-shot .45 or a fifteen-round 9mm. (I prefer to call it an ammunition reserve, not firepower.) But he won't stop there. He will carry a spare magazine. The gunner with a .45 will often carry a spare seven-round magazine, slim enough to fit just to the side of his wallet in the left-rear pocket. The fellow carrying a SIG or Glock may not find this carry comfortable and will probably forget to carry his spare, although he may opt for a lightweight magazine carrier. I am aware that quite a few gun writers claim to carry two spare magazines for their semiautomatics at all times, but I have yet to meet one in real life. I think one spare magazine is the limit for civilian carriers. Most cops I know who carry the high-capacity semiauto—standard around my part of the country, in either 9mm or .40—carry a single spare magazine on duty, with the occasional fellow carrying two. Those carrying three spare magazines are looking for a mighty deep creek!

I mentioned the quickest reload—carrying a spare handgun. I adopted the backup .38 and carried it for more than twenty years. I did not carry spare ammunition for the .38. This was a last-ditch tool, not a frontline combat handgun. On the other hand, when going on a raid or dangerous patrol, I often carried two full-size pistols, not always a pair of 1911s, but often a 1911 and a Browning Hi-Power. With one carried in a crossdraw, either was considered first-line depending upon the position I was in, when and if I would be called upon to draw. In that case, I always carried a spare load for the second pistol. I think we should carry a spare load for the handgun, but barring a nervous breakdown and uncontrollable shakes of the trigger finger, a single load should be adequate. A palm reader may give a better prediction, but mine is based on experience. I was once on the hit list of an organization affiliated with so-called American Nazis. There is an oxymoron, as everything America stands for is the opposite of the Nazis' warped ideology. For several weeks, I carried two full-size self-loaders. It worked for me, but in the heat of the summer, it was quite uncomfortable. There was no gunfire, but I did manage to wreck an Oldsmobile Toronado full of Nazis.

There are reasons other than running out of ammunition for carrying a spare gunload. First, after the festivities are over, we wish to replenish our handgun to its previous capacity. If one or two or eight rounds were fired, we will wish to reload the handgun. We are then ready for the next situation that may come along. Second, we may experience a malfunction and need to clear and reload our piece. The classic TAP, RACK, BANG malfunction drill will cure most problems, as true jams are rare. But sometimes the spare magazine may need to be ripped out, the slide locked to the rear, and a fresh magazine inserted. Without a spare magazine at the ready, we are in trouble if we have a bullet-over-the-feed-ramp malfunction. Practicing malfunction clearances is important with the semiauto, as they can occur at the most inconvenient times. I maintain that the first three to four shots will decide the action, and the semiauto allows swift, accurate delivery. If your man is not down, or you have not gotten to cover with the first few rounds fired, your battle may be over. If you have a malfunction, you must clear it quickly. With the revolver, five or six shots may be cutting it close in a deadly encounter, so carry a spare load. Revolver malfunctions are so severe, they can seldom be cleared on the spot, but reloading after the action is always an option.

Several gun writers favor carrying spare ammunition, because we may vary the ammunition we fight with. The first two rounds in my revolvers are Glaser Safety Slugs, followed by hollow points.

Carrying a spare gunload of ball ammunition for the .45 or 9mm may make sense if felons behind cover are part of your likely scenario, but for the most part, modern hollow-point loads penetrate as well as ball against light cover. (*Police Magazine* published a report about vehicle penetration that showed the Hornady 124-grain XTP .357 SIG load was the single most effective handgun loading against vehicles. I am familiar with the situation as it was my report.)

Hollow-point loads are hotter than ball ammunition on average. While military-issue 124-grain NATO 9mm is a hot load, most commercial full-metal-jacket ammunition is intended for practice. Once the soft nose of a jacketed hollow point is smashed shut on meeting metal, it actually penetrates deeper than an FMJ bullet. I once knew an officer who carried two rounds of

Glaser, two to four rounds of Winchester Armor Piercing, and numerous hollow points on his duty belt. I can understand the slow, deliberate step of inserting the Glaser to safely dispose of an injured animal on crowded urban streets. But how anyone could remain calm enough to choose alternate ammunition needed in a fight is beyond me. We cannot agree on the reasons, but we can agree that we should carry spare ammunition.

Carrying spare pistol magazines is easy; they are much slimmer than the handguns they feed. A magazine carrier can be thin and unobtrusive. While inside-the-waistband carriers are available, I find a single carrier on the belt is just as concealable under a pulled-out shirt if the magazine is carried high enough. Even a dual pouch is fine with the slim 1911 magazines. Glock, SIG double column, and H&K magazines become a little hairier to conceal, but good carriers that set the wings or belt loops away from the magazine, producing a pancake effect, can work.

Speedloaders for revolvers are another matter, because they can be about as thick as the gun. Such a device may fit OK in jacket pockets, but a pouch is traditionally worn on the right side, in front of the revolver. Perhaps one that looks like a tobacco pouch would work for concealed carry, but most are a bit difficult to conceal. The JOX Loader Pouch carries the speedloader high on the belt, producing better concealment with little loss of speed. Belt loops and pocket carriers are obsolete. The position of the speedloader or spare magazine carrier is dictated by the proper execution of drills in reloading the handgun. With that in mind, let's move to learning proper speedloading techniques with either type.

About forty years ago, I learned revolver drills and mastered the semiauto a bit later. Along the way, I questioned whether the time and effort was worthwhile to improve speed loading. No extra ammo will help if the initial shots missed the target. Over time, I have met several animals that needed a full gunload to expire and collected quite a few case studies of human adversaries who behaved much the same. Experience shows the speed load should be practiced.

It is a difficult acclimation to become used to carrying a handgun, then add a spare magazine carrier. But there are reasons for carrying spare ammunition beyond the obvious. It stands to reason we should learn the quickest way to recharge our firearms in order to make use of these spare loads. Nothing I am saying changes the advice I have given—shoot straight and do the business in the first few shots fired. But worst-case scenarios do occur.

SPEED-LOAD TECHNIQUES

The Revolver

To execute a revolver speed load, first transfer the revolver to the weak hand and open the cylinder.

After the revolver is fired empty, the strong hand transfers the revolver to the weak (usually left) hand. In doing so, the strong hand hits the cylinder

The muzzle of the revolver must be perpendicular to the ground, and the ejector rod must receive a good, sharp rap to eject the spent cartridges.

release. The weak-hand fingers press the cylinder open, while the thumb strikes the ejector rod. The muzzle is pointed straight up to avoid a case-under-the-ejector malfunction as the spent cases are ejected. The strong hand draws a speed loader from the strong-side carrier, as the weak hand orients the muzzle of the revolver toward the ground. The speedloader is moved to the cylinder. The fingers extend to the cartridge-case nose to properly guide the speedloader.

Manipulating the speed loader by the release knob is the wrong technique. The cartridges are inserted, the release knob is twisted, and as the cartridges fall into the cylinder, the speed loader is dropped. The thumb of the support hand presses the cylinder shut as the strong-side hand grasps the handle, and you are ready to fire again. It is important that the speed loader is guided by a forward grip on the device and not simply grasping the release knob. The proper technique is much steadier. Keep your fingers extended to

The revolver is now loaded and may be put back into action.

The speed loader is used to load the cylinder.

the edge of the bullet nose and guide the bullets into the cylinder.

If you are left handed, a modification is needed. You will transfer the revolver to the right hand, which then opens the cylinder. Then, the revolver is transferred back to the left hand, and the speed load continues as with the right-handed person. The left-side, swing-out cylinder of the revolver demands this modification, but allows the lefty to carry his spare ammunition on the right or opposite side. An alternative is to use the left hand to press out the cases and then draw a left-hand-mounted speed loader, but this is generally slower. Remember, most left-handed shooters are far more adroit with the right hand than right-handed shooters will be with the left, as this is a right-handed world.

Moon Clips

Another option for revolvers is moon clips. Usually in .45 ACP caliber, there are also 9mm versions and custom variations, including the .38 ACP Super. When the cartridges are carried in the moon clip, all are ejected during the drill in a positive manner. The revolver need not be pointed upward. The cartridges are carried in the steel clips in one unit. When reloading, the drill is the same as with a speed loader, but more positive. The likelihood of a cartridge-under-the-ejector malfunction is eliminated. The only drawback is that most of these revolvers are large, .44 or .45-frame handguns.

Semiauto Drills

This drill is the same with practically every semiauto. The pistol is held in the firing hand throughout the drill. Left-handed shooters will modify the drill

The automatic is fired to slide lock.

The free hand moves to grasp the spare magazine.

The spare magazine is angled from the magazine carrier and toward the pistol.

The magazine is angled inward when loading.

The magazine is slapped home.

The magazine is always fully seated with the palm of the hand.

by pressing the magazine release with their forefingers—no further changes are needed. The shooter notices the piece is empty when the slide locks to the rear. The thumb presses the magazine release, allowing the spent magazine to tumble to the earth. At the same time, the weak-side hand is rushing to the magazine carrier worn just forward of the hip on the weak side. The forefinger goes down the body of the magazine, stabilizing it as the magazine is drawn. Magazines are carried bullet nose facing forward. The magazine is inserted in the magazine well. The magazine is angled in, meeting the back of the magazine well, and angled into the magazine. The magazine need not be slapped into place; it will lock with firm pressure. The slide lock may be activated or the rear of the slide grasped, pulled to the rear slightly, and released. I prefer the latter method, as it is surer under stress.

Modifications

There are pistols in use with the heel-mounted magazine catch. Modify the drill to include releasing this catch. With the HKP7M8, the cocking lever is activated after the magazine is seated, dropping the slide. Know your individual handgun!

An alternate to using the slide lock to release the slide is to grasp the rear of the slide and release.

At this point someone will probably ask what is the fastest of all pistols to reload. Despite the fact that I have many years of experience with the 1911, I find the Hi-Power slightly faster, except perhaps for those 1911s I have fitted with a Smith and Alexander Magazine Guide. The Hi-Power fits the hand so well, it is simply lovely to handle, and the high-capacity magazine is funneled at the top for easy insertion into the magazine tunnel. The advantage over a SIG or Glock is in the tenths of seconds. Hardly a deal breaker for personal defense, but pretty important in competition.

I have spent endless hours practicing the speed load. On the range I often fire my handguns empty and execute a speed load to keep my hand in. While practicing, I draw as quickly as possible and execute a single shot with maximum accuracy. But there is always a final shot. In the end, carrying spare ammunition is cheap insurance; time spent practicing the reload adds to familiarity with the handgun, increasing your smoothness of manipulation. That is always worthwhile.

CHAPTER SIXTEEN

MULTIPLE ADVERSARIES

Many shooters practice for personal defense by firing at a one-dimensional target they are squared to at a distance of seven yards. There is no thought given to cover. The time interval to address threats is generous—fifteen seconds for five shots is common. This isn't training. At best, this is an elementary exercise for beginners; at worst, you are simply making brass. Among the real problems that must be addressed in training is the possibility of multiple attackers.

You must be prepared for the likelihood of facing more than one gunman. Wolves, dogs, and sharks run in packs. So does our protein-fed, ex-con criminal class. In many scenarios, the chances of multiple assailants are the rule. It is a psychological constant that gang animals will do things collectively that the individual would not do. Their depravity is multiplied by several factors.

There are a number of important aspects of this problem that are vital to understand. When you are outnumbered, there are five critical steps that will determine your survival. There are a number of subcategories that also bear attention. For example, a rapid presentation of the firearm is vital. Choosing a proper holster for daily use is practically as important; your skills cannot be gained with a third-rate holster.

I hope you have chosen a service-grade handgun of 9mm or larger that you are able to control. The homework must be in place for the basics to proceed to advanced drills—there is no shortcut. Here are the five most important means of learning to handle multiple assailants:

When faced with multiple adversaries, the first impulse is to hose the threats down with fire.

We must fire accurately to stop each threat; ammunition is precious when facing multiple threats.

You must fire accurately and address one problem at a time when firing at multiple adversaries.

1.   **Develop situational awareness**
2.   **Practice tactical movement**
3.   **Master the presentation**
4.   **Learn proper gun handling**
5.   **Master marksmanship**

SITUATIONAL AWARENESS

Situational awareness begins with the decision that you will not go through life asleep. The ability to think a few seconds ahead is a precious asset. You must be secure in your ability to quickly assess a situation and observe street conditions. You must be able to size up those individuals in close proximity and develop a well-tuned sense of threat avoidance.

There are troublesome situations that should be avoided. If the worst case does occur, and you end up facing multiple adversaries, then the awareness of your surroundings will help you determine their position, how they are armed, and their movements.

TACTICAL MOVEMENT

Tactical movement is perhaps the single most important, life-saving action. When the moment occurs, it isn't like the whistle at a 3-Gun match. You will be caught up in what has been aptly described as the "Tyranny of the Moment." Your heart will be beating heavily, your eyesight and hearing may be affected, and complex thought and actions may not be possible. Tunnel vision often occurs. Your performance will default to the average in training. You will not rise to the occasion and perform beyond what you have achieved in practice. Too many rely upon skills they are unable to demonstrate. Prior training is the greatest predictor of survival in a gunfight, so train well. If possible, take the high ground. This simply means sidestep out of the line of attack, take cover, or if possible, redirect the attack. Back to rule one—if there is cover nearby, and you are aware of this cover, take cover! Or consider a variation of the martial arts tactic called "shielding"—the art of quickly subduing one of the attackers and using him to shield against the rest of the gang.

When moving and firing, sometimes only one hand may be used. Be certain you have skill in one-hand fire.

Shielding would come into play if two or three assailants are attacking shoulder to shoulder or spaced at lateral intervals. This is common. While generally applied to open-hand combat, gunfights also occur at close range, and assailants are often armed with blunt-impact weapons. By sidestepping and moving to the side of the assailants on the far left or right, you may reduce their ability to attack in unison and address the threat one at a time. While shielding may not apply to every incident, it is a tactic you should know.

Another consideration in tactical movement is often overlooked. There is a great difference between police, military, and civilian shooters. The military man usually has other soldiers with him. Police officers caught in bad situations are usually alone, but often surrounded by citizens. A citizen may have the family along. This is fertile ground for discussion.

There are two schools of thought. One states that you should move your body in front of the family member you are protecting, and this may be the first impulse. Like the Secret Service, we are willing to take a bullet for the principal. I think that if the attack is by assailants armed with edged weapons or their fists, this is a viable move. However, special units over the world use

If possible, move when facing multiple adversaries and practice shielding.

another tactic. They have reasoned that covering the principal with your body simply means that you will draw fire.

Rather, moving toward the threat as you fire will force the threat to concentrate on your actions and not attack the family member. The British Special Air Service was highly successful in using this tactic against the Irish Republican Army. Perhaps moving away from the family would be the superior tactic if paired with return fire.

PRESENTATION

Gun Handling

Gun handling is an ability to smoothly holster, draw, fire, and reload the firearm. This enhances your ability to fire on the move. With constant practice, this isn't as difficult as you might think. The drill is to quickly move to one side and then pivot and fire as soon as you are stationary. At close range, this tactic works well for those who practice.

If you must reload, and the adversaries are not down, make it fast!

So, practice hard. If you don't, drawing on the run may result in an awkward pantomime. Gun handling is everything in a short-range battle.

MARKSMANSHIP

Institutional figures show that most police agencies have about a 30 percent hit rate in critical incidents. A very few agencies with intensive training programs have posted a 50 percent hit rate. A person at the same skill level faced with two adversaries will have to fire six shots minimum to make two hits. With decent shooting skills and a 9mm or .38-caliber handgun loaded

Most of us begin our practice firing from right to left if we are right-handed.

Often, we must incorporate some type of judgment call into firing at multiple targets. Vary the drill, perhaps hitting the middle target first, then left and right, and then change up for the next drill.

Firing accurately, quickly, is the only means of dealing with multiple threats.

with +P ammunition—a realistic minimum—there is no room for error. You must handle and run the gun efficiently and be competent with stoppage-clearance drills and have the ability to fire off hand or from cover.

At close range, marksmanship is just as important as firing at a threat fifteen yards away—perhaps more so, because the threat doesn't need good skills to inflict damage at a short distance. Tactical movement and a smooth presentation are wasted if you do not have good marksmanship skills. You will lose everything if you jerk the trigger and do not maintain the sight picture. There will be innocents nearby in many situations, and you must fire accurately. The proper trigger press, sight alignment, grip, and follow-though must be practiced.

If you have to slow your cadence of fire to get a hit, then you must, because there is no excuse for a missed shot. Consider this—in a fistfight you will be punched. You will be cut in a knife fight. Chances are good you will be

It is important when outnumbered to seek and use cover.

shot in a gunfight. You want to land the heaviest blow first. A strong punch in the arm isn't very effective. Move that strong right hook to the jaw, and you might flatten your opponent. A blow to the throat might kill him. Where the bullet strikes is of the greatest importance.

HOW TO PRACTICE HITTING MULTIPLE TARGETS

The presentation must be swift and sure when facing more than one opponent, and when facing any opponent. Move into the firing stance, and deliver accurate fire.

The author fires the El Presidente often, although it is modified for his use.

I like to run the El Presidente drill. Is it realistic? No. But it teaches movement, marksmanship, and gun handling. When you are able to run the El Presidente in ten seconds with all of the hits in the kill zone, you are ready for advanced drills.

Set Up

Post three targets, shoulder to shoulder, at ten yards. (Seven yards is OK for beginners.)

When beginning the El Presidente, the hands are raised.

The drill begins with the shooter's back away from the targets. Pivot and face the three targets. Draw; fire two rounds at each target. Reload, even if you have a high-capacity handgun. The point is to build reloading skills. Fire six more rounds. This is a challenging, skill-building drill.

Is one attacker more important to stop than the other?

Of course he is. If the adversary closest has a knife, and another behind him has a pistol, shoot the closest first. How about if two are equally apart from you, but one has

Turn and fire two rounds in each target, reload, and execute the drill enough when performing the El Presidente.

a shotgun? The shotgun is deadlier. The main thing to do is engage quickly. Hesitating while identifying the weapons is not as important as getting into action against armed attackers. Let's face it—stopping a single adversary is difficult enough. You have much less time when addressing multiple opponents. The time frame is so compressed, you do not have a spare moment for an inaccurate shot! Practice often for this problem.

CHAPTER SEVENTEEN

DIM-LIGHT AND LOW-LIGHT SHOOTING

The truth about low-light shooting and personal defense is simple. When you are found in a situation in which you must fire, the basic skills in place will give you an edge in survival. The presentation, the draw, the stance, and body positioning will carry the day in a low-light encounter. If you cannot see the sights, you will be in the same position with the same grip and stance as if you could see the sight.

In dim light, or any light at all, you should be able to see the front sight. You will then adopt the close-quarters battle technique of placing the front sight on the adversary's belt buckle. This is good for short range. At longer ranges, you need a better sight index. I am more about tactics and rigorous

Learning to address steel plates quickly and accurately remains a positive reinforcement for multiple-threat engagement.

training than hardware, but one item that is not a gimmick and that I do not consider optional is a good set of night sights. While white outline and three-dot sights work well for most of our dim-light shooting, they do not work well in all dim-light shooting. It is better to have night sights and not need them than to need them and not have them.

For many of us, our shooting began before night sights and before portable but powerful flashlights. We went about with a flashlight in hand not much smaller than a ball bat! Today, the pocket flashlight is highly useful.

Much has been written concerning weapon-mounted lights and their uses in dim light. For most of us, the weapon light will seldom be present when we are engaged in a defensive battle. Very few of us will carry a handgun fitted with a weapon light in a holster. Peace officers may be conducting a building search or raid and have the handgun in hand with the light mounted. (It is a poor choice to use the handgun and light as a search tool. It is a combat tool.) The defensive encounter takes place in a few seconds. You will not have the time to draw both gun and light and plug them together.

On the other hand, the pocket light is a very versatile tool. You may sweep a parking lot or look for dropped keys and even check the rear seat of the vehicle for unwanted hitchhikers before entering. The light isn't

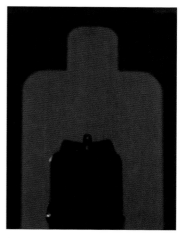

This is the dim-light sight picture when using XS sights.

confrontational and doesn't announce you are armed. The pocket flashlight is a tool we should all have.

In my experience, the weapon light is best when attached to the home-defense handgun. Illumination and identification are vital in a home-defense incident. The weapon-mounted light supplements the handheld light. Today, handheld and weapon-mounted lights may put out 300 to 500 lumens, excellent for most any encounter. Few of them use bulbs; most use the superior diode. But the bottom line remains skill.

When you are engaging an adversary in dim light, your peripheral vision will be limited. Muzzle flash is also a concern. In my experience in experiments, muzzle flash does not affect vision to the point the sights are not visible, but muzzle flash does affect vision to the point a target is more difficult to locate and identify. Some loads are less offensive than others. The Winchester Law Enforcement loads often exhibit little muzzle signature, sometimes only a warm glow. Well-balanced loads will demonstrate a full powder burn. Muzzle flash is simply unburned powder. Powder that does not combust in the barrel burns outside of the barrel. Magnum-revolver cartridges sometimes produce a bright ball of flame. There are sparks from the ejection port of an automatic and the barrel cylinder gap of a revolver. So, muzzle flash is always present, but in different degrees. As a rule, high-intensity cartridges using larger amounts of relatively slow-burning powder produce the most muzzle flash. The .45

ACP usually produces a few sparks and, even with +P loads, only a warm, orange glow.

While most gunfights occur rapidly, and body positioning and aiming work well for combat at three to five feet, it is also good to learn to marry the combat light to the handgun. The light should be powerful enough to be useful.

You should practice the Harries Flashlight Technique. The flashlight is deployed in an ice pick-type grip, with the handgun held in the strong hand

and the light held with the diode facing out the bottom of the support hand. The thumb is on the button-type light switch. The non-shooting hand crosses under the shooting hand. It is vital that the support hand is kept far enough to the rear so that the hand never crosses the muzzle. The back of the support hand is hard against the back of the firing hand. The thumb operates the momentary switch when it is desired to illuminate and identify the subject.

The Harries position is shown, with the combat light in one hand and the Commander .45 in the other.

Remember, never point a gun light, mounted or not, at anything which you are

The light and the handgun are used together in the Harries drill.

The Harries is a proven formula that works well in low-light situations.

not justified in pointing a firearm. Practice the skill of combining illumination with the firearm, and you will be able to defend yourself on a twenty-four-hour basis. You must practice firing with the light held in the Harries position. This isn't as solid a firing platform as the conventional two-handed hold, but it works well for those who practice. And it is a short-range tactic. You can practice in daylight, as the primary focus is learning the Harries. Be certain that the hand crosses under the handgun and that at no time is the support hand near the muzzle of the handgun.

Retention is also important in dim light; this is a combination that would work well during a search. The Harries may be quickly assumed if need be from this position.

Another technique seldom practiced is marrying the retention position to the combat light. There is no good reason to walk around with the handgun and the light at maximum extension. If the adversary is hidden and waiting to pounce, he may make a grab for the handgun. The handgun may be kept in the retention position, and the combat light, held in the support hand, may be used for illumination. If the adversary is at greater range, the Harries position may be taken quickly. If he is at contact range, you will be glad the handgun is in the retention position.

A BUMP IN THE NIGHT

What will you do if your home is invaded? What if you hear the bump in the night? The time to decide isn't when the door is kicked open at three o'clock in the morning. You must have an answer before the event. Since I work at home, my security plan is applicable on a twenty-four-hour, around-the-clock schedule. Within the week, I have been surprised by a number of individuals going door-to-door with various sales pitches and cons. We

Some firearms accept lights, but some do not. The ability to mount a combat light isn't a deal breaker for the author.

This is the proper means of actuating a combat light. This is the grip that must be used to marry the light to the handgun.

recently suffered a rather damaging storm that could have been much worse, but the result was an influx of the occasional craftsman looking for honest labor and the crook looking to con us. We have also seen door-to-door salespeople in our home county, and the sheriff's department alerted us about their old sham trick. Others were the usual door-to-door evangelists/cultists attempting to steal my faith. Amid these are the usual delivery people and our lovely elderly neighbors. The sorting out of guests, unwanted and welcome, requires some mental gymnastics. I do not wish to greet the UPS man at the door with a Colt Commander in hand, but then I do not wish to present an invitation to the con using a sales pitch as a prelude to a home invasion.

For example, I was pretty concerned with a power outage last week during a storm. Our neighbor came knocking to inquire about the power situation. David is 88 years old and a wonderful neighbor. So, I am pretty used to guests and need to be certain that I am not lulled into complacency. I hope you won't be called upon to repel boarders. But a glance at the news will confirm that the possibilities are endless. It is always better to read the news than to be the news. We have to consider the statistics. Statistically, the most likely event occurs at night. Thieves like the cover of darkness, and they prefer to invade an unoccupied home. Sometimes they make mistakes; sometimes a takeover robbery is the plan.

For the homeowner, the ideal plan involves retreat to a safe room. When children and dependent individuals are in the home, you must ensure their safety first. And while calling 911 must be part of the plan, we cannot await the arrival of the cavalry. As simple as it may seem, the first thing to do is wake up; there isn't a lot you can do or should do without full awareness. Carefully approach the problem. Clear your mind before you implement the plan. Proceed with caution. There are worse things than being shot, and one of these is shooting the wrong person. Clear your head and then break the problem down into incremental steps to be addressed.

There are many good combat lights available, and none are terribly expensive.

The Sphinx 9mm is shown fitted with the Viridian combat light, a compact but rugged unit.

Upon hearing the alarming bump, grab your handgun, shotgun, or rifle, and the bedside light. Do you have a capable combat light beside the bed in easy reach? It isn't just the home invasion that demands such a tool; practically every type of problem and emergency demands illumination.

With your weapon and the light, begin cautiously to clear the

The revolver and the combat light may be used together by a skilled shooter. Be certain that the support hand doesn't lie in line with the barrel-cylinder gap. The ejecta will sting, at the least.

bedroom, and then the adjoining rooms. Be certain that no one is in the room with you. Keep the handgun close in the retention position so that you are not easily disarmed. If you are not alone, alert your partner or spouse. They can more easily return to sleep than be caught unaware.

Move carefully to clear the rest of the home. Always maintain distance. Do not become a target indicator. Do not stand in the middle of the hallways, but, rather, remain close to the walls, presenting as small a silhouette as possible. Do not travel past any room you have not checked. It is little good to rush to the nearest outside door if the felon is in the opposite bedroom. Remain as calm as possible. If you have practiced this drill, you will be calmer than if you had not trained. It is easy to crouch or hyperextend your arms to the point that blood flow is restricted. A calm thought pattern and proper stance will go a long way toward a successful outcome.

When searching, think a second or two ahead. Consider what may be around the next corner.

If you are familiar with the term "slicing the pie," you understand how to clear a room or a house in sections. It doesn't matter how long it takes, what matters is that it is done safely and thoroughly. Study first one section of the suspect area then another. Carefully clear each room or hall, and do not leave a section to your back that you have not cleared.

While a felon may attempt to hide, in my experience of making police reports over the years, the most common reaction is to flee. The worst type of felon attempts to assault or kill you to escape. If you hear a sound, it is time to illuminate with the handheld or weapon-mounted light. At this point, be certain that the target is a threat. Within the year, the media has carried reports of various home invasions by the usual drunkard, doper, or criminal, but also break-ins by the homeless. In one case, a victim fled from a violent criminal; in another, a victim ran from a deer that burst through a glass door. The odds are in your favor, but the possibilities are endless.

A powerful handheld light is a great addition to the handgun for the person who understands its use.

If you are confronted with a threat and must fire, accuracy is essential. A volley of shots should be avoided. If there is more than one home invader, which seems to be the trend, you may need those shots. Fire as accurately as possible. This is the worst-case scenario, but we should train for that. You should practice clearing your own home. Be certain you are aware of obstacles and the placement of furniture. The life you save may be your own.

Dim-light and night combat are serious concerns, and as you may gather from my emphasis, most likely to occur in the home.

CHAPTER EIGHTEEN

ROUND OR SQUARE GUN?

The Smith & Wesson .357 Magnum double-action revolver (top) is a proven firearm. So is the Beretta 92 9mm (bottom). The self-loader is more efficient, but the revolver has its merits.

The topic of revolver or semiautomatic pistol is debated nearly 120 years after the introduction of the first reliable self-loading pistol. Are revolvers obsolete? In a very real sense, as first-line combat handguns, the revolver has not been in its heyday since 1911.

However, the Mexican Revolution kept the Colt Single Action Army in use twenty years past its prime. Although the FBI and various agencies used the 1911 self-loader as a substitute standard in the 1930s, the majority of peace officers carried revolvers. Stark reality finally prevailed against an obdurate mindset, and the American police obtained self-loading handguns in wholesale measure beginning in the early 1980s.

As far as accuracy, control in rapid fire, rapid reloading, and even reliability, the self-loader is superior to the revolver. The single niche that the revolver outshines the self-loader is in the backup gun category. The snubnosed .38-caliber revolver is a useful handgun with advantages to be considered, but it requires considerable effort to make it worth deploying. For most of us, the modern, high-capacity self-loader is the better choice.

One must be certain that the chosen handgun matches ability, desire to practice, and other situations. This book is concerned with personal defense, not pest control or hunting. A rancher who wishes

The .45-caliber revolver (top) is much bulkier and more difficult to conceal compared to the .45-caliber self-loader.

Self-loaders are relatively flat. Even this service-size .40 may be concealed in a Don Hume IWB holster.

The Beretta 92A1 features a seventeen-round magazine and mounts a combat light.

to keep his hands free during his chores might prefer a quality .357 Magnum revolver. It will take out a marauding coyote well past fifty yards. I will not argue the point. But, if this rancher faces a dope gang lurking on his property, does he wish to defend himself with a handgun that requires considerable effort to recover from recoil?

It has been thirty years since the widespread adoption of the self-loading pistol in police circles. We no longer hear of cops gunned down because their revolvers ran dry. It is almost laughable to attempt to keep up the pace with the application of revolver speed loaders.

In any honest comparison of the two types, the self-loader has superior accuracy, particularly for backup shots and multiple shots. It also offers the ability to quickly address multiple targets and allows a trained shooter to reload quickly.

There are many well-practiced shooters who can reload a semiautomatic pistol in two seconds or less with practical, street-proven handguns. This is important, but not as important as building the skills that result in hits with the first few shots.

How much time do you have to spend on the revolver reload? I hesitate to mention speed in the same sentence with revolver reloading. The time spent practicing this reload could be spent with another skill-building exercise. There is some utility in a revolver for home defense, as the system is simple. The revolver may be left stored for months without maintenance and still come up shooting. I cannot argue this point.

But the revolver was issued for so long to peace officers, because they were half-trained shooters. For most of the twentieth century, training was doled out incrementally in yearly sessions. Often the yearly qualifications featured no training at all, and the drills were not difficult. The double-action revolver was a reasonable choice. But I think that the impression of a need for greater training time with the self-loader may be an insult to the intelligence of shooters. In my training classes we have gotten shooters up and running with the self-loader with a few hours of instruction, as far as state-mandated requirements are concerned. Distance education and careful study are great aids.

This .44 Special revolver hits hard and features a smooth action. There is much appeal to this system. The grips from Culinagrips.com make a great difference in handling.

As long as the safety rules and operating procedures are understood, the self-loader presents no great obstacle in adoption. The rapid trigger reset of the self-loader coupled with the ability to control the type in rapid fire are advantages not easily ignored.

There is a considerable argument in favor of the more powerful revolver cartridges, but with modern ammunition, this argument is less valid. Prior to 1935, the accepted means of increasing a handgun's wound potential or stopping power was to increase the size of the bullet. The .45 Colt's 255-grain bullet

Sometimes it boils down to ammunition reserve. The .357 Magnum revolver (top) carries six rounds, the 9mm self-loader (bottom) fourteen rounds.

makes it the largest practical personal-defense cartridge. Yet the .45 Colt is scarcely more effective than the much more compact .45 ACP cartridge.

In 1935, the .357 Magnum revolver was introduced. The new precedent was increasing velocity to achieve greater killing power against game animals. The .357 Magnum enjoyed some popularity with police forces, but the revolver was large and bulky. Later, small-frame Magnums were not long lived in service due to the pounding of the cartridges. Just the same, the .357 Magnum enjoyed a good reputation for stopping aggressive attackers with a single shot.

There was some contention among professionals, with the .357 Magnum worshipped by one group and the .45 ACP by others. The self-loader was obviously the more efficient, which was bore out with the winning use of the

1911 pistol in every type of competition. But the competing schools received a new facet of performance, of which many are still trying to get a better understanding.

Beginning in the late 1960s, with progress continuing steadily until the present day, bullet design became ever more important. Given sufficient velocity to instigate expansion, plus a well-designed bullet, you did not necessarily need high velocity and a heavy bullet for reliability. While common sense tells us the big bore is more efficient, the effectiveness of proven loadings such as the .38 Special +P and the 9mm Luger +P+ cannot be disputed.

Today the .357 Magnum is loaded to about the same pressure level as the 9mm +P, making the Magnum less attractive. Then there is the popularity of the .40-caliber cartridge. The .40 neatly bridges the gap between the 9mm (small bore) and the .45 (large bore) with few downsides. When it comes to big-bore handguns, only the self-loaders are of a manageable size.

The large-frame .41, .44, and .45-caliber revolvers are too large for most hand sizes to control efficiently during rapid fire. They may be fired accurately enough in slow, deliberate fire, but that is not sound personal defense. These heavy revolvers are also slow in presentation from the holster. This leaves us with little recommendation for these revolvers in a personal-defense setting.

When concealed carry is considered, the semiautomatic is the hands-down choice. Even the blockiest of the self-loaders are thinner than a revolver's cylinder bulge. I realize there are shooters who still rely on the revolver. An acquaintance of mine is a retired highway patrolman and a fine shot. He recently qualified with a perfect score with his heavy-barrel Smith & Wesson .38-caliber revolver. That is the choice he began service with and something he understands and trusts. But there is no reason to limit yourself if you desire to have an efficient and capable defensive handgun.

I am a student of the great writers of the previous century. During the 1930s, Ed McGivern came to the forefront as an exhibition and speed shooter. He carefully discussed the

The .38 snub-nosed revolver (top) is the more reliable backup and hits harder than the .380 ACP pistol (bottom).

Single Action Army and noted that while good in its day, that day was gone. Yet, many lawmen carried the SAA until the 1950s. Perhaps they were aware of the feats of arms of George S. Patton, Douglas McArthur, and others in Mexico. Or they may have been contemporaries of Tom Threeperson. If you feel the same concerning the double-action revolver, then you can save your life.

Note spent case in the air. The 9mm self-loader is controllable even with the heaviest loads.

The double-action revolver offers an advantage in a smooth, rolling trigger action. When firing heavy loads, the smooth, surprise break seems to limit flinching due to anticipation of recoil. The .44 Special and the .357 Magnum are available in relatively light, fast-handling revolvers. They are viable. We do not all get to the range enough to practice. Even time for routine lubrication and cleaning is at a premium. The self-loader must be cleaned and lubricated, whether it is fired or not, a point lost on some users.

While the self-loader may be more difficult to maintain than the revolver, even old-school handguns, such as the Browning Hi-Power, are simple to field strip.

I cover several of these points in the chapter on snub-nosed revolvers.

A final point—while we are primarily concerned with defense against human adversaries, in many parts of the country animal attacks are a possibility. The big cats and feral dogs are real problems. The attack is usually very fast, often bowling over the victim. The revolver may be pressed into the animal's body and fired repeatedly, but the self-loader would jam at the first shot. Those recommending the 10mm or .460 Rowland semiautomatics for animal defense are really talking about hunting and don't realize the difference between hunting and defense use of the handgun. The animal may have you down before you can fire. If you travel often in the wild, and animal defense is a concern, then the double-action revolver is the best choice. The

The .357 Magnum revolver is a potent instrument. For those willing to master the revolver, the K-Frame Magnum is a viable choice.

caliber should begin at .357 Magnum and build from there, depending upon the shooter's competence. Solid, non-expanding bullets should be used.

The self-loader remains the best choice for rapid deployment, running combat drills, facing multiple adversaries, and concealment of a powerful handgun. But the revolver will serve if the shooter is well trained.

CHAPTER NINETEEN

SNUB-NOSED REVOLVERS

The snub-nosed .38 Special revolver isn't a target gun. It isn't useful in competition, although there is an IDPA category for the short-barreled revolver. It isn't a hunting handgun, but I have taken small game with the snub-nosed revolver. The primary category for this gun is life saver.

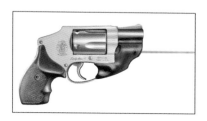

A neat combination: the snub-nosed .38 and Lasermax laser.

On practically a daily basis I receive e-mails, letters, and calls asking me to describe the ideal defensive handgun. Many of these people are harried with jobs, families, and busy lifestyles. They simply have little time to devote to mastering the handgun. This isn't ideal, but it is what it is. Life often has harsh demands. We must maintain a certain amount of proficiency, but we do not have to choose the most complicated gear to do so. A weapon that is easily secured, simple to manipulate, and strikes a hard blow may be the best choice. The double-action, .38-caliber revolver has fit that role for almost 100 years.

The snub-nosed .38 is typically recommended for novice shooters as a carry gun, but experienced shooters often carry it. It's simple to manipulate: just press the cylinder release, swing the cylinder out of the frame, and load the revolver. Close the cylinder. Press the trigger to fire. To unload, press the release, point the muzzle in the air, and tap the ejector rod. The .38 is light, handy, and powerful; it responds well to a trained shooter. Perhaps more so than any other handgun, the .38 gives up its best results for those who practice and master it.

Just 1-7/8 inch of barrel adorns this Smith & Wesson 442, yet it will get the job done.

BASICS

There are two basic types of snub-nosed .38s—five-shot and six-shot revolvers. There are also large-frame revolvers that have short barrels, but they aren't true snubs.

This is among the smoothest and most accurate revolvers ever built, the Colt Detective Special.

The five-shot version is the most common and the revolver most of us will deploy. There are aluminum-frame and steel-frame models. There are versions with a concealed hammer that is hidden in the frame. These revolvers may be fired double-action only. In other words, the hammer may not be cocked for a deliberate shot. While the hidden hammer revolver is generally considered the superior revolver for personal defense, good work may be done with conventional double-action types. The concealed-carry revolver is less likely to snag on the clothing during a draw.

By carefully practicing the double-action trigger press, good accuracy may be had. With a single-action option, there is always a possibility of taking a deliberate shot at long range. Cocking the hammer for a single-action shot isn't recommended for personal defense, but if the felon is at the long end of the hallway firing around cover, the single-action press may be a strong option.

Six-shot revolvers are compact enough for personal defense, but they are belt guns, while a five-shot revolver may be a purse or pocket gun. Recoil is less with the steel-frame handguns. These revolvers weigh around twenty ounces, while the aluminum-frame handguns weigh fifteen ounces, depending on the exact grip type and other considerations.

The six-shot Colt Detective Special is now out of production. With modern, hand-filling grips the Colt weighs about twenty-three ounces. With respect to the laws of physics, the heavier handguns kick less. Aluminum-frame revolvers are controllable, provided they are fitted

The Smith & Wesson 442 concealed-hammer revolver is, in the author's opinion, the finest lightweight .38 ever manufactured.

with hand-filling grips. At best, they become uncomfortable during long firing sessions. I fit Ahrends grips to my snub-nosed revolvers to enhance control, hand fit, and comfort.

TRAINING AND OPERATION

Several rules make snub-nosed training time beneficial and speed progress. First, practice the double-action trigger stroke in dry fire with an unloaded firearm. Keep the front sight on target as the trigger is carefully pressed to the rear. The cadence of fire is: press the trigger in a smooth operation until the revolver fires, let the trigger reset, and press again. During the double-action firing stroke, the front sight should not move off the target. Press, reset, press, reset. Even after you have considerable time in with the revolver, this practice regimen should be followed.

A laser sight is a great aid in training. When you are pressing the trigger, watch the red dot on the target at three, five, and seven yards. When you begin practice, the dot will bounce all over the wall. When you have mastered firing the handgun, the double-action trigger press will be smooth and the dot more or less stationary. Practice drawing from concealed carry, and practice firing at very close range. Also practice the retention position. An advantage of the revolver in close-range battle is that the revolver may be pressed against an adversary's body and fired time after time. A self-loader would

The snub-nosed .38 may be fired from the pocket in a worst-case scenario.

After ripping through a jacket pocket, the snub-nosed .38 remains ready to fire again.

jam. You should also practice the combat reload as described in the chapter on speed loading if the snub-nosed .38 is your primary weapon. There are excellent speed loader pouches available from JOX Loader Pouches that maximize concealment with a low profile, but offer a rapid draw.

AMMUNITION

Although it is increasingly difficult to find target-grade, 148-grain full wadcutter, this cartridge is an excellent training resource. With light recoil and good accuracy, this load allows training to proceed quickly. Black Hills Ammunition manufactures a quality rendition of this classic load. The new Winchester Train and Defend 130-grain, full-metal-jacket load serves at a fair price. Both are accurate and burn clean.

In personal defense, the problem isn't finding a credible load—it is finding one that is controllable in the snub-nosed .38 format. With non-expanding ammunition, the .38 Special has demonstrated questionable ability to stop a motivated felon with a minimum of shots. However, a .38-caliber bullet that expands will create a wound channel that produces more damage. The only reliable mechanism of stopping an adversary is actual damage. Among the loads that have fared well in my personal testing are the 110-grain loads from Cor-Bon. Although both the conventional hollow point and the

The Galco strong-side holster, combined with the snub .38, is a brilliantly fast combination into action.

There are a number of interesting ammunition variations on the .38 Special for both practice and personal defense.

all-copper DPX loads are loaded to +P pressure, the relatively lightweight bullet makes for good control. The primary component of stopping power is marksmanship. These loads give the shooter armed with a .38 Special revolver a fighting chance.

CONCEALED CARRY

The snub-nosed revolver is short and compact, and can be carried in a number of holster designs. Because the barrel is short, the holster must retain the handgun by pressure on the cylinder. I have tested the 3Speed holster extensively, not only with the snub-nosed .38, but also variants made for the self-loader. This holster is surprisingly comfortable. Yet, when properly worn inside the pants in the appendix position, both speed and concealment are good.

With any revolver, practice trigger control and trigger reset to master combat accuracy.

After firing through a jacket pocket, the S&W 442 is ready for action again.

Many choose to carry the snub-nosed .38 in the pocket. I have used several pocket holsters with good results. The Rinehart Leather version, with a flourish of embellishment, has served well. I have used the Barber Leather Works pocket holster with good results. Be certain to ask the holster maker if the garments you normally wear are side-loading or top-loading pocket types.

The Jason Winnie Leathergoods inside-the-waistband holster is a classic, double-loop holster with much to recommend it. For

The 3Speed holster has given excellent results in daily testing and carry.

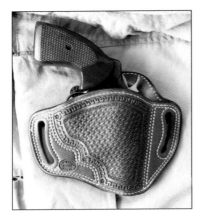

The D.M. Bullard holster for this Detective Special offers a true Western basketweave with an excellent balance of speed and retention.

The author's modest battery of working .38s includes the Smith & Wesson 442 (left), and the Colt Detective Special (right). Note JOX speed-loader pouch and HKS speed loaders.

those favoring a strong, single-belt clip, the Cover6 design has given good results. When covering garments are worn, these IWB holsters are a good choice. For those who cannot acclimate to the IWB technique, the strong-side holster from Jason Winnie has much merit.

GRIPS

Some revolvers have grips that are too small for comfortable use. Ahrends tactical grips solve a lot of problems for the snub-nosed .38 and comfort. A number of grips are too short for some shooters to get their hands completely in control of the guns. Available for the Smith & Wesson J-Frame revolver, the Ahrends Banana grip neatly solves this problem. The grip is extended past the revolver frame and offers a good purchase while firing heavy loads.

When drawing the snub-nosed .38 from concealed carry, you will find no handgun gets faster into action. The generous grip and short barrel means that there is plenty of leverage for a rapid draw. Shoot the elbow to the rear and scoop the handgun from the holster. Be certain the grip is affirmed when the revolver is still in the holster. Bring the handgun to the front of the body, meet the support hand, and press the handgun toward the threat.

The snub-nosed .38 is short and easy to maneuver, even inside of a vehicle. Plus, the hand-filling grip and short barrel enhance retention. The felon has little to grab, while the trained gun handler maintains control of the grip.

Practice hard, choose support gear wisely, and the snub-nosed .38 will prove a viable option. If you can carry a larger and more powerful handgun, you should. But if you are comfortable with the snub-nosed .38 Special, and it fits your needs, who am I to criticize? When you need a backup handgun, the snub .38 is the best bet.

Postscript: Among the original big-bore conversions to a short barrel was the Fitz Special. The reasoning behind the piece is interesting and still has merit almost 100 years after the first Fitz Special, developed in the mid-1920s by J.H. Fitzgerald for Colt. He took a full-size service revolver, bobbed the hammer spur, cut the barrel to two inches, and sheared off the front part of the trigger guard. This led to Colt's factory Detective Special. The short barrel allowed rapid handling inside of a vehicle, which was becoming important in the 1920s. The only short revolvers available were not as reliable as full-size revolvers and fired pitifully ineffective cartridges. The short-barreled revolver took gun handling over target shooting. That isn't a bad thing today.

CHAPTER TWENTY

SERVICE GUNS AND CARRY GUNS

If you are in law enforcement or the armed services, you will be issued a handgun. Cling to that gun, train with it, maximize its advantages, and minimize the shortcomings. But there is a difference between service guns and carry guns. The baseline of power and reliability should not be compromised, but size, weight, and capability are fine-tuned in the carry gun.

The SIG P226 Navy Model is among the most proven and capable handguns in the world.

Civilians may deal with armed gangs, but multiple, heavily-armed adversaries, felons behind vehicle cover, and prolonged gun battles or running gunfights intertwined with car chases are not part of our scenario. The battle will be finished within a few seconds. However, there are exceptions you should be prepared for.

If you are a soldier or peace officer, then your practice must have no limits. As for the difference in handgun size and capability, Sam Colt defined this more than 150 years ago. He offered

Glock offers belt, concealed-carry, service, and tactical-grade handguns.

handguns in holster, belt, and pocket sizes. Everyone understood the sizes and capabilities. Today, a service pistol, personal-defense pistol, and pocket pistol fill the same well-defined roles Sam Colt envisioned. Service handguns are full-size guns chambered for service calibers, including the 9mm Luger, .40 Smith & Wesson, or .45 ACP. There are many similar, competing designs. As examples, the Glock 17, HK VP9, and Smith & Wesson Military &

Note bumps under the slide lock to prevent the firing hand from interfering with the slide lock. The compact Glocks also feature slight thumb swells on the grip. The handguns are well thought out.

Police 9mm fill the same tactical niche, so do the Beretta 92 and SIG P226. There are differences in trigger actions and the various hand fits that people prefer. The designs are similar—the bottom line is that there is little that may be accomplished in a tactical sense with one over the other. Glock versus HK or SIG versus Beretta, tactically you are a formidable shooter if you have mastered the handgun and practice with it consistently.

The single most important decision when it comes to gear is choosing a quality handgun. There are a number of police and military tests that may guide you. The Ohio State Highway Patrol tested nineteen handgun types, ten examples each, and chose the SIG P226 DAO in .40 caliber as standard issue. This involved a rigorous 228,000-round test program. The FBI also subjected handguns to a demanding test program and chose Glocks for general issue and the Springfield 1911 .45 for SWAT use. Each went through approximately 20,000 rounds in reliability

Government Model Colt, case in the air, and back on target. Service-size handguns are controllable.

These compact handguns from HK and Smith & Wesson have been proofed with a wide variety of loads. They are service-grade in reliability.

testing. The French police tested a number of handguns in a 700,000-round program. The single handgun equipping all police and military units in France, with a twenty-year contract, is the SIG. The Beretta 92 won the U.S. Military handgun competition. In Europe, the CZ 75 has won similar exhausting competitions.

The Colt Combat Elite is among the best 1911 Government Model handguns the author has tested.

The original Colt 1911 won the military competition in the year 1911, firing 6,000 trouble-free rounds in a demanding contest. The Smith & Wesson Military & Police revolver served American peace officers for decades without a complaint as far as reliability. These handguns are proven, service-grade choices.

It isn't difficult to take a design and cut corners to make it cheaper. Some of the value-line handguns are fine for recreational shooting, but they won't endure an exhaustive test program. During my classes, I have seen various "bargain" revolvers fail with cycling problems and locked-up actions. Quality firearms are not inexpensive. Proficiency at arms is purchased with a different coin. When you consider what you will spend on training and ammunition over a decade of use, the difference between a cheap gun and a first-class pistol is inconsequential.

The Glock 19 is the pistol to beat in 9mm compacts. This example has fired thousands of practice loads and never malfunctioned.

Glocks should be the baseline of expense. The various models are around $400-$500, but you can spend more on added features. Glocks are reliable and combat capable. If you spend less, you may not get a reliable handgun. If you spend more, the features should warrant the extra expense.

The best choice in caliber for most shooters is the 9mm. Larger calibers are more difficult to control, but at the least, the beginner's gun should be a 9mm. Ammunition is plentiful, and there are effective loads available. As I will discuss in the chapter on ammunition, the 9mm isn't the most effective cartridge, but it is a reasonable compromise between control and wound potential.

Mastering a heavier caliber requires considerable effort and regular practice. The service-size handguns may be concealed using modern holster designs. However, some people find that the bulk of a service pistol is uncomfortable to carry. A viable alternative is a compact version of the gun. The slide and grip are shortened to make a smaller package. The SIG P229 is the compact version of the P226, and the Glock 19 is a smaller version of the Glock 17.

The little-known Beretta 92A1 compact is the author's favorite Beretta and a great all-around defensive handgun.

There is also a less well-known compact version of the Beretta 92. The HK 2000 is another reputable compact. The Smith & Wesson Military & Police self-loader is available in several frame sizes. These pistols are excellent all-

The SIG P227 .45, in the author's opinion, is among the two or three best service pistols in the world.

around, concealed-carry handguns. Many are found in police and military holsters.

The compacts are faster from leather than the full-size handguns. Most fit small hands better due to the S curve inherent in shortening the grip. The short sight radius may limit absolute accuracy at twenty-five to fifty yards, but these handguns are more than accurate enough for personal defense. They are the ideal size for all-around personal defense.

The Glock 19 in 9mm is widely regarded as the best balanced of all Glock handguns. On the firing range in difficult drills, the Glock 19 gives up little, if anything, to the Glock 17.

The Glock 19 (top) and the Glock 23 (bottom), one in 9mm and the other in .40. The 9mm pistol is among the easiest of all compacts to use well. The author prefers the .40, but each is a great handgun.

I prefer the harder-hitting .40-caliber Glock 23, but the Glock 19 is a great handgun.

The author's personal SIG P220 Carry Elite with Viridian combat light is a remarkably accurate and reliable handgun.

Among the most advanced compact versions of a service pistol is the SIG P220 Carry Elite. It is shorter than the proven P220 and has a redesigned grip frame to offer an upswept tang for comfort in .45 caliber.

In researching this book, I wished to isolate several standout handguns that I could recommend for the modern shooter. I do not wish the book to become dated in a few years, but there are always new introductions. Measure them against proven handguns that have track records.

Among the handguns best suited for duty use is the new SIG P227 high-capacity .45. It is as good a service pistol as exists. But for concealed carry, I would not care to lug the P227 unless I had to. The SIG P220 Carry Elite is a different matter. With the smooth SIG action and target-grade accuracy, this is a first-class handgun. With the reliability of the SIG P series and the hard-hitting .45 ACP cartridge, this handgun is a winner on every count. I have fired more than 1,000 rounds in working this handgun out and find it a first-class defensive weapon.

A Smith & Wesson M&P compact (left) and the Beretta Storm (right), each in .40 caliber. They proved difficult to control during the author's testing.

In 9mm handguns, I kept coming back to the Glock 19. There is no better balance of portability and effective performance. I also tested FNH's FNS-9 handgun and found it tactical, accurate, and reliable. HK handguns are famously reliable.

There are smaller handguns that may be considered. They fall into two broad categories. These are subcompact service pistols and purpose-designed compacts. The

Glock 26 and the SIG P250 subcompact are examples of abbreviated service pistols. Purpose-designed subcompact pistols include the Kahr K9 and Walther PPS. In my experience, the abbreviated service gun variants are the most useful and reliable. A very good compact pistol is the Smith & Wesson Shield, a single-column magazine version of the Military & Police 9mm. This is a controllable and accurate handgun that I have tested extensively.

Before choosing a subcompact for daily use, consider your options. In my hands, the Glock 19 is as controllable and accurate as the Glock 17. The Glock 26 represents a more difficult pistol to use well by a margin. The Glock 19 is fast from the holster and fast on target, but the smaller Glock 26 is more difficult to draw due to less grip to grasp and the short sight radius; combined, these factors limit speed on target.

Abbreviating the grip frame and slide are beneficial to a point, after which we face a point of diminishing return. The smallest handguns are useful as backups or when concealment is at a premium, but you are better served with the compact pistol versus the subcompact pistols. Remember, I am not saying the smallest guns are uncontrollable or inaccurate, far from it. Some, such as the new Glock 43 in 9mm,

Among the finest choices in a hideout 9mm is the Smith & Wesson Shield.

are pleasant to fire. The larger guns are simply more comfortable to shoot and easier to control.

THE 1911

The 1911 design in quality renditions from Colt, Kimber, SIG, and Springfield is a good choice for service and defense use. While I respect the reliability and low maintenance requirements of other pistols, some are a triumph of the technical over the tactical compared to the 1911.

The 1911 is a single-action design. The trigger does only one thing, and that is drop the hammer. The 1911 features a straight-to-the-rear trigger compression. Its bore axis rides low over the hand. This results in limited muzzle flip. The combination of a low-bore axis and straight-to-the-rear trigger compression, with a relatively light let off, results in the most controllable of the big-bore handguns.

The 1911 must be carried cocked and locked, hammer to the rear, safety on. The safety locks the hammer. A grip safety locks the trigger in place until the grip safety is pressed. Each safety is easily addressed when the pistol is held with a natural grip. If you loosen your grip or drop the pistol, the grip safety is activated. The grip of the 1911 fits most hands well.

If you adopt the 1911, you must be dedicated to learning the manual of arms and practicing it diligently. The recoil of the .45 ACP cartridge is not something a person of average strength and stature will have a problem with, but the recoil is greater than the 9mm. The pistol also demands frequent cleaning and lubrication—even if it has not been fired, it must be lubricated for best reliability. Lubricant tends to run off of the pistol toward the muzzle.

I would never carry a 1911 based on someone else's recommendation or because it was expected of me. I carry the 1911 because it has proven the best tool for the job in my hands. Carefully consider your level of commitment and dedication to training. When you choose the 1911, you will note that there are a lot of versions of it. Many are made cheaply; others are made to sell as the primary goal. I have tested many handguns. Some publications seem never to have found a gun they did not like.

This isn't true at *Gun Tests* magazine, and quite a few of the handguns I have tested are found wanting; the "1911" stamped on the slide isn't a stamp of acceptance. If the pistol is clean, lubricated, fed quality ammunition, and the shooter isn't causing the problem, then something is wrong with the handgun.

There are several rules concerning the 1911, but the first is to purchase a quality handgun, not a bargain-basement product. I prefer the 1911, but I would carry a Glock or a Smith & Wesson Military & Police self-loader over a cheap 1911. The recommendations for the 1911 are many, and some refer to the treatment of quality handguns as well as the cheap ones.

First, do not attempt any type of gunsmithing beyond the scope of your knowledge. Second, change recoil springs when they have lost a portion of their free length, no matter what the round count. Check the plunger tube and spring. The 1911 plunger tube must be staked in place properly, and the spring and indent must be good in order to keep the slide-lock safety and slide lock working properly. Often a seemingly inexplicable problem is actually the result of a slide lock that rides against the slide, causing a malfunction. The nose of 230-grain, hardball ammunition may even contact the slide lock and cause a problem. There is a rule that the more junk on the gun, the less it works. Do not use recoil buffs on a carry gun. They may slow down pounding for range work, but also impede the slide's fully rearward travel.

Eight-round magazines should be loaded with seven rounds only, no matter what the man says! When doing a press check with the fully loaded, eight-round magazine, you will note more pressure on the slide as it is moved to the rear. The fully loaded, eight-round magazine is difficult to slam into the frame and lock when the slide is locked forward. Again, use the seven-round magazine or load the eight-round magazine with seven rounds.

Given a quality, well-lubricated 1911 with proper ammunition, you have a reliable platform. But owner incompetence has ruined many good 1911 handguns.

REVOLVERS

There are advantages to the revolver we have discussed. Simplicity of operation is one. The best all-around choice for personal defense is the Smith & Wesson K-Frame revolver chambered in .357 Magnum, with a four-inch barrel. The Ruger is indestructible but larger and heavier.

Fixed sights are preferred for carry use, but many users prefer the sight picture offered by Smith & Wesson adjustable sights. The red-insert front sight found on many Smith & Wesson revolvers is also popular.

Practice with the .38 Special is recommended to master the .357 Magnum. While I respect the opinion of trainers who say the load that is carried, or a load of the same power level, should be used for practice, I respectfully disagree in this case. In a defensive confrontation, we will fire a minimum of rounds. Twelve to eighteen cartridges would be a war. We may fire eighteen rounds of .357 Magnum in practice before recoil blunts our ability to shoot accurately. On the other hand, a box of fifty .38s may be fired in practice to allow the shooter to acclimate to the trigger action and sights. It is the difference between practicing for thirty minutes with a punching bag and then stepping into the ring with a hard-hitting sparring partner. Each is beneficial.

A few Magnums will allow you to know what to expect and be certain you may control the revolver. With proper technique, you will be able to use a K-Frame .357 Magnum well. If you are leery of the Magnum, but prefer the revolver, .38 Special +P loads are roughly comparable to 9mm Luger +P loads. The .357 Magnum, however, outstrips either for wound potential.

The four-inch-barreled .357 Magnum revolver is a formidable defensive handgun. Performance is enhanced with quality grips. Hogue makes them for Smith & Wesson revolvers, including the MonoGrip, which is ideal. The Ahrends custom grip is even better. Older revolvers will need new grips to reach their full potential.

The small-framed, five-shot revolver chambered for the Magnum cartridge is another matter. These guns are nice at handling .38s, especially if they have heavy-barrel underlugs and good grips. But, when loaded with the Magnum rounds, they are very difficult to control. The small parts take a beating.

I examined one that had fired fewer than 300 rounds, but the ejector-rod retaining lock was so battered that the piece would not open. The man who owned the gun said it was terrible to shoot, yet he had given it to his wife to use. She carried the gun with Magnum loads and had never fired it!

The short barrels of these revolvers do not develop enough velocity with the relatively slow-burning powder used in .357 Magnum cartridges. Most of them should be avoided. But the most manageable of the small revolvers is the Ruger SP 101. This rugged Ruger is a good choice for those who favor a snub-nosed Mangum, and it seems never to give trouble.

The big-bore revolver is usually too large to be seriously considered for concealed carry. I have known a few men who have carried one version or the other of the Smith & Wesson N-Frame, with fixed sights and four-inch barrels. The .41 and .44 Magnums are too heavy at close to fifty ounces loaded. Smith & Wesson produced a retro line of the revolver with a pencil barrel and fixed sights. They seem to be out of production but, just the same, are plentiful in new-in-the-box condition from retail outlets. They were, unfortunately, supplied with ridiculously small grips for this design's round-butt frame. But, with a set of Culina finger-groove grips, these revolvers are comfortable to fire. They also feature the new transfer-bar ignition.

The .44 Special is a good choice and hits hard with Cor-Bon loads. The .45 Auto Rim version may use .45 ACP cartridges, clipped into moon clips, making it the most efficient of any revolver to reload quickly. These revolvers offer proven wound potential and reliability beyond question. They are reasonably fast from leather with practice and offer a good option for those who prefer the revolver and cannot manage the self-loader.

OTHER CHOICES

In the lighter class of handguns in 9mm, I have tested most of what is available. I have found both the Ruger LC9 and the LC9S reliable. The Springfield XDS compact 9mm handgun shoots as well as most big guns. The Walther PPS is more compact but doesn't handle quite as well as the XDS. There are many tradeoffs, but these handguns have proven to be reliable. They simply are not as effective on the range as the Glock 19 and similar handguns, but then that is no surprise, the laws of physics being immutable.

If you think I am giving the .40 a short shrift, it is because I have seen many students show up with handguns they simply could not control, and the majority were .40-caliber compacts. One young man was so hopeless, I simply could not let him continue the course with that handgun. He missed a man-sized target at ten yards and jerked the trigger with every shot. In this case, the 9mm is much more controllable and the better choice. But, in a trained hand, controllable .40-caliber handguns include the Glock 23 and the smooth and accurate SIG P229.

A pistol that was introduced as I was finishing this book is the Glock 43 single-stack 9mm pistol. After some 350 rounds in one example and more than 100 rounds in another, I find the pistol reliable, accurate, and useful. This is the pistol to beat in its class.

I have mentioned that only the 9mm +P or the .38 Special should be considered the minimum calibers for personal defense. The .380 ACP and the .32 H&R Magnum are inadequate. In the past, the small self-loaders were, for the most part, unmanageable and unreliable. But, while I consider the wound ballistics inadequate, there are .380 ACP pistols that have proven reliable and accurate and would make good backup pistols.

One is the Glock 42. Glock has managed to forge a handgun that is not

The author has found the Ruger LC9 S a good performer within the limitations of its size.

only reliable, but also quite accurate. Recoil is mild. As a backup handgun loaded with the Cor-Bon DPX load, the Glock 42 has merit. I strongly prefer the .38 Special for backup, but the popularity of the .380 ACP pistol demanded a test. Anytime I find myself siding with the majority on any question, whether it is political, religious, or regarding popular handguns, I feel the need to engage in strong self-examination! As it turned out, the little Glock is a great handgun—save for wound ballistics. The Glock 43 9mm is much preferred.

Another exceptional small pistol is the Kimber Micro Carry, a .380 that is a joy to shoot and handle, and surprisingly accurate. The power deficit is all in the wrong direction, and I have no confidence in the caliber, but these Kimbers are well made and reliable.

THE BOTTOM LINE

I would never carry a handgun for personal use below the .38/9mm baseline, nor would I deploy a gun I consider uncontrollable in rapid fire. The handguns that have seen widespread institutional use—the Glock, the SIG, the Beretta 92, the Smith & Wesson Military & Police revolver, and the Colt Government Model 1911, the Springfield 1911, the SIG 1911, and the Kimber 1911—enjoy excellent reputations. There are models that fit most hands well and chamber acceptable cartridges. The man or woman behind the gun is most important, but these are good guns to stand behind.

CHAPTER TWENTY-ONE

THE CONCEALED-CARRY LIFESTYLE

A weight-loss plan and physical training are important lifestyle changes. The concealed-carry lifestyle is also a difficult adjustment, but one that is worthwhile and respectable. You are taking charge of your own safety. Concealed carry is a lifestyle, because it embraces a belief system and cannot be taken lightly. It's something to grow into with serious study. Carrying a handgun isn't just something you do. It isn't like jogging or driving a car or preparing a meal. It is an outlook. You must carefully think it through with research and training.

The author has set up a training scenario in which he is confronted by a threat at the market.

Responsibility and commitment come with the lifestyle. If you wish to own a handgun only to scare or intimidate people, and do not think you could pull the trigger, then a cap gun will suffice. If your lifestyle includes doing stupid things with stupid people, you do not need to add a handgun to the mix. Even cops sometimes get into trouble when they behave stupidly off duty. The end result is well deserved, whether a suspension, fine, or jail time.

When you are carrying a gun, you must be aware of its presence at all times. When driving, at work, or in the shower, you must know exactly where the handgun is and who has access. You should be the only person with easy access to the handgun at all times, whether awake or asleep. When you carry a handgun, you have taken responsibility for your own safety. You have also accepted the challenge to train and act lawfully so that you don't endanger the community.

Getting a concealed-carry permit is the goal of many people, but this is just the beginning—an administrative step. The training delivered from state to state varies, but most of the courses cover a few hours. Much is compressed into these courses, with the legal aspects the primary goal of the teacher. These are important; ignoring them could adversely affect your life. Much time is spent in every class addressing ridiculous assumptions, urban myths, and falsehoods brought up by students. Pay attention, double-check behind the instructor, and have a good understanding of the laws governing concealed carry. But that isn't living the lifestyle; that's simply the necessary preparation.

If you have the handgun and the permit, then you must have made the decision to defend yourself and others. Carrying a handgun concealed at all times isn't easy. Your lifestyle, mindset, and clothing require adjustments to the new mantra. You cannot lose control of the handgun. How often have you read in the news that someone—either a cop or armed citizen—left their guns in the bathroom at a restaurant? Or worse yet, they suffered an accidental discharge? Adroit handling and awareness of a gun prevents such debacles. Losing a lethal weapon is quite a bit worse than losing the wallet or cell phone, frustrating as either may be.

The greatest adjustment is carrying the handgun while maintaining a balance of speed, access, and retention. And it must also be concealed at all times.

When carrying concealed, only the best load-bearing devices work for those wishing to carry serious gear, such as the CZ 75 pistol. This Nightingale Leather holster is an excellent all-around concealed-carry holster.

The concealed-carry lifestyle begins with a commitment to education.

This doesn't mean a tight shirt over the handgun, revealing its bulge. This doesn't mean the barrel is protruding beneath a light windbreaker. This means that the handgun is concealed, not concealed so well that you would pass a security frisk, no, but concealed from the casual observer. When you are walking, the pistol should not look like a water moccasin that swallowed a possum riding on your side. The butt should not "print" against the outer clothing.

This is perhaps a perfect outline of a pistol under a shirt! This is printing, and even the best gear will print if you bend deeply.

Printing is a term that describes the visible outline of the handgun or holster pressing against the outer clothing. This must be avoided. When you bend over or stoop at the grocery store, bend at the knees, not the waist. Develop a means of moving that does not print on the outer

When wearing the pistol, stoop—don't bend—to avoid printing the outline of the holster.

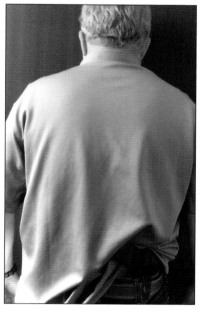

If you allow the covering garment to roll up over the handgun, it is just plain sloppy and may have more serious legal consequences than an unzipped fly.

clothing. This won't be hard if you chose a holster that is properly fitted to the handgun, belt, and your clothing. To do otherwise is amateurish.

Once you have become acclimated to the handgun, you will not be hyperaware of it, but you must never forget that you are armed. When you go to a restaurant, store, or take a walk in the neighborhood, the handgun is always at your side. To be armed only by the situation is foolish. Do not strap the handgun on because you are going to make a night deposit or run to the ATM after sunset. Either may not be the most tactically sound move you could make even when armed. If we all had clairvoyance and could predict danger, we would find ourselves either, A, in the next county when trouble goes down, or B, armed with a Colt AR-15 rifle.

While freedom-loving folks are galled by such signs, the law is clear. We must obey.

This inside-the-waistband holster from Jason Winnie offers an outstanding balance of speed and retention. The dual belt loops make the holster a solid companion, rather than a chafing nuisance.

Only by carrying the handgun at all times will you be prepared for the unexpected. This is what concealed carry is all about, although the term brings confusion to the uninitiated. You do not carry the handgun only at times, but *at all times*. There are quite a few businesses that post signs that say "no concealed handguns" allowed. Of course this means that they do not want my business, and I do not give it to them. Unfortunately, there are times when entering such a place cannot be avoided. More reasonable is leaving the handgun behind when we enter federal buildings, like post offices. After all, this property doesn't belong to the state that regulates your concealed handgun; rather, it belongs to the federal government. Never break the law; do not carry when proscribed by law. This

CHAPTER TWENTY-TWO

HOLSTERS, BELTS, AND SUPPORT GEAR

Any tool needs load-bearing gear when the tool is not actually in use. The handgun must be carried in an accessible location and stay relatively comfortable while concealed. This is a tall order. The balance of speed and retention is essential. The handgun must always be rigidly held in the holster. It cannot flop about, and it must be firmly attached to the belt at all times (as per the Concealed-Carry Lifestyle chapter). You must be aware that the firearm is on your person. The handgun cannot be exposed to public view at any time. I am continually surprised by people who show up at training classes with cheap, inappropriate holsters that are actually dangerous. More than one student has attended class with a good handgun and a ten-dollar holster. Others have bought gimmick holsters not suitable for personal defense. Some students purchased holsters to be worn under the shirt or buried in the pants, but they never practiced the draw. Consequently, they couldn't realize how poorly designed the holster is or how difficult a presentation would be.

A properly designed and executed holster will enhance how you defend yourself. The handgun will be accessible, and you will be able to re-holster with one hand. As an example, a well-fitted holster that hugs the body and the belt, such as the Avenger design from Drew Dog's Holsters and Leather Craft, allows the carrying of a heavier handgun than perhaps you would have thought comfortable. A poorly designed holster

This Drew Dog holster exhibits the essential elements of a concealed-carry holster: excellent double stitching, a reinforced holstering mouth, and good fit to the individual handgun.

This colorful, custom piece from SAS holsters is among the best of the breed in Kydex. It is both rigid and rugged.

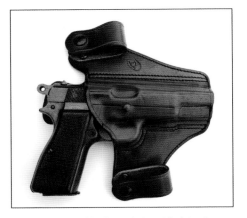

This custom, inside-the-waistband holster from Nightingale leather exhibits excellent craftsmanship. Note double stitching and strong belt loops to offset the weight of a service-grade handgun.

will allow the handgun to sag, which accentuates the weight of the handgun. A holster should keep the handgun rigidly in place so that the draw is smooth and the handgun offers the same resistance to the draw each and every presentation. The strong-side scabbard in Kydex from SAS Custom Holsters allows a degree of personalization and meets these criteria.

A concealed-carry holster should never rely upon a strap to keep the handgun secure in a soft holster. By the same token, a holster worn inside the trousers should never rely upon body compression to keep the pistol secure. As an example, carefully examine the tight "boning" of the IWB holster from Nightingale Leather. This holster will not accept any handgun other than the specific model it is molded for. Boning refers to the practice of working wet leather and using a smooth bone to fit the holster to the handgun. Some are more tightly fitted than others; many makers offer several models of holsters with progressively tighter fits. This type of handwork is expensive. As may be expected, the tighter the fit the longer the break-in period. A custom-grade holster is a good thing to have and well worth the price.

A junk holster will become a chafing nuisance. Quality holsters are not inexpensive, but there are factory products that are more than acceptable. Galco is a custom maker that employs many artisans. Galco holsters are excellent and arguably the leader in off-the-rack quality. As of this writing, a good-quality holster may be had for less than $100. The sky is the limit with custom jobs, and good Kydex holsters will run about $65.

It is true that enthusiastic handgunners will often opt for exotic leather. Sharkskin, lizard skin, and elephant are popular. The sharkskin holster from D.M. Bullard Leather has many good features. While the design is excellent, the sharkskin component limits wear to a minimum. Scuffs are easily polished out, and sharkskin locks rigidly into a shark-skin belt.

Those on a budget can find good-quality gear at a fair price. Don Hume Leathergoods offers workmanlike design at a fair price. The first duty holster I wore was a Don Hume. They are still a good choice with modern designs. If you feel your handgun is like a soulmate and wish to invest in a top-flight exotic holster, do so. But less expensive, quality holsters are available.

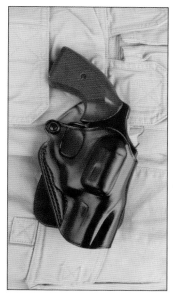

GALCO offers off-the-rack, custom quality.

It seems to be a modern trend to offer holsters with embellishments, from simple initials to elaborate artwork. This is all to the good, as we have been embellishing our gear and weapons to our personal tastes for thousands of years. This gear must be workmanlike, however. Holsters remain in states of development, with new models emerging from popular makers.

This IWB, from Ted Blocker, offers a strong steel belt clip and a workmanlike thumbreak.

Ray Cory is a former deputy chief of police and respected designer. His Combat Classic belt scabbard is among the best designed and executed holsters examined in the process of working up this chapter and evaluating modern holsters. The heavily reinforced construction and excellent boning results in a holster with a balance of speed and retention, which are both excellent. Western saddle makers pioneered the art of holster making, and Cory is among the best of the breed.

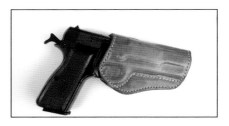

Lobo Gunleather's newest design was evaluated for this book and found excellent.

A holster should never be stamped with something like, "Size 6—fits several models." Perhaps for a beginner's range holster, within the limits of the range, these holsters are OK. But they should never be used for personal defense. The holster must be secure against a normal range of daily activity. A good test is to jump up a few times to test retention. For example, more than fifteen years ago, I was knocked over a piece of living-room furniture while carrying my handgun in a Galco Royal Guard IWB holster. The pistol did not budge, and I was able to recover and resolve my problem.

The holster should separate the gun from the body. The sharp edges of the handgun should not be allowed to gouge the body. The handgun should be protected from corrosive body salts. It doesn't take long for perspiration to begin to interact with the handgun's finish. Even the Glock and a stainless Colt have small parts that are subject to rusting. The Eagle Defender from Nelson Holsters offers a well-designed sweat guard that protects the body from the edge of the handgun and, to an extent, also leads the handgun into the holster as the piece is sheathed. I ordered mine with the optional two-tone support. This is a good design from a talented maker.

Nelson is a new name in gunleather but a very good one.

Some like an open-top holster without the sweat guard. The Jason Winnie Leathergoods design, illustrated with the Smith & Wesson Shield 9mm, offers the fast and unimpeded draw some prefer. The sweat guard has utility, but also represents personal preference.

Jason Winnie's pancake is well turned out. Speed is excellent with this holster.

The holster should be constructed from quality saddle leather, not soft-suede leather. Horsehide is stronger than cow leather and allows a thinner holster; the exotics cannot be thinner but offer advantages in resistance to wear and scuffing. Some are resistant to moisture. Kydex holsters are impervious to oil, solvent, and moisture. They should be .065 thick for best rigidity. Few of us will be served well by a single holster, although some, such as the Wright Leather Works' Cobra, are very versatile. This holster serves as a capable double-belt-loop IWB holster. But the leather support wings have belt loops that allow the holster to be worn under a light shirt in the IWB mode and under covering garments in the OWB mode. Few dual-purpose holsters work well, but the Cobra offers good service in either use. Most of us living in an area with a true four-season climate will

The Wright Leatherworks Cobra offers excellent utility. It may be used as an OWB or IWB holster.

need a minimum of two holsters to serve our year-round needs. While a single IWB may work across the board, when we are able to wear covering garments, the speed and comfort of the belt holster are good to have.

The strong-side holster is never a bad choice. This holster offers a natural draw and rides high enough on the belt line for comfort. There should be a good reason for leaving the strong-side holster behind. As an example, the Kydex holster from ZZZ Custom Works offers good retention by contact with the long surfaces of the handgun. The holster is secure, and speed is excellent. ZZZ also offers one of the best appendix-holster designs in the world. The optional goatskin backing for comfort should be specified with this holster.

There are times when the strong-side holster isn't concealable. That's when the IWB and the appendix holster are useful. Any system should include a hard look at allocation of belt space. All of us have approximately a yard of belt space. The belt will serve to secure the holster, a

ZZZ Custom Kydex offers service-grade gear with a good balance of speed and retention.

spare magazine carrier, and perhaps a cell phone carrier and key ring. The holster will be on the strong side and the carrier on the non-dominant side. If you deploy a revolver, the speed loader pouch is carried on the same side as the gun, toward the front of the belt. The goal is to be as familiar with the handgun as you are the cellular device you use every day. The gear must be arranged so that one accessory does not conflict with the other. Many amateurs place items on the belt in a manner that is inaccessible when engaged in normal movement. I have seen magazine carriers worn toward the middle of the back and so close to the holstered handgun that the draw and accessing the carrier would conflict. Practice in rapidly accessing the handgun and also the spare ammunition supply is required. Do not adopt a carry mode that limits your access or rapid presentation.

STRONG-SIDE HOLSTERS IN FOCUS

There are several types of strong-side holsters, including the Avenger, the scabbard, the pancake, the belt slide, and the paddle. The Avenger is possibly the most secure and the fastest. This holster features a belt loop that cinches the holster in tight by running the belt close to the trigger guard. The holster is heavily stitched and designed for speed and retention.

This rust-elephant rig from D.M. Bullard is both breathtaking and combat capable.

The scabbard is similar and offsets the holster from the body for a sharp draw. The pancake is designed to hug the body. Original pancake holsters were basically modified belt slides. Often they were not tightly boned and did not have a level of retention that most of us preferred. The modern pancake, such as the one illustrated from Defensive Line Leathers, is a different matter. The Avolto rides tight to the body but features strong stitching that effectively separates the holster from its supportive backing. The Avolto features a holstering welt that

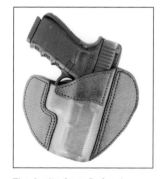

The Avolto from Defensive Line Leathers offers a high ride, good molding, and brilliant speed.

reinforces the mouth of the holster and a sweat guard as well. There are simpler pancakes but few as well executed.

Jason Winnie grew up learning leather-working from his grandfather, Don Hume. Jason has taken the pancake holster and improved it by a notch or two. Well stitched and offering excellent retention, the pancake holster Jason created also offer a thumb-break version for those who want extra retention. A number of police agencies specify that off-duty officers must use a thumb-break holster. The Jason Winnie design is as good as it gets. Be certain to practice rapidly disengaging the thumb break. Jason's design falls easily under

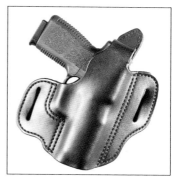

This pancake holster from Jason Winnie offers a reinforced thumbreak.

the draw as you execute it, and it's rigidly molded. I prefer the other models from Jason's shop for concealed carry, but the thumb break is so well done I had to highlight it. When hiking with the cocked-and-locked 1911, I deploy Jason's thumb-break pancake holster; it's ideal when the occasional slip or fall occurs.

The belt slide is a rather simple holster that carries the handgun by pressure on the slide or cylinder. The pistol slide or revolver barrel extends from the belt slide. I see this holster as primarily a range holster for use during practice. However, several makers offer a modern belt slide that is well stitched and properly blocked and molded. These holsters offer greater retention than the original belt slide. Rine-hart Leather makes them. Clover Rinehart

Rinehart leather offers holsters that are not only eye-catching, they also work well for practical use. These pancake holsters spread the weight of the handgun about the belt while offering a fast draw.

has earned a reputation for quality holsters with affordable, custom embellishment. A holster is personal, and the logos and personalization are important to some of us. Clover's belt-slide holsters are well suited to short-slide handguns. The molding is good, and the draw is fast. Be certain that the combination you have chosen does not protrude so far below the belt slide that the muzzle contacts a chair when you sit and levers the handgun out of the holster.

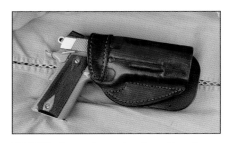

Wild Bill's Concealment Leather offers the Fusion paddle for concealed-carry use. There is no better paddle-holster design.

The paddle holster can be controversial. Some do not like the level of retention. It is true that many of the early designs featured a belt hook that was far from secure. The design was intended to give peace officers a holster that was easily removed quickly, which would appeal to officers who had to remove the holster often while entering secure areas. When interviewing prisoners, as one example, the handgun was removed and placed in a locker. Modern holsters, such as the Fusion Paddle from Wild Bill's Concealment, feature secure locking to the belt. The paddle spreads the weight of the handgun on the body, offering a degree of comfort. The offset of the paddle affects concealment. However, a close-riding paddle holster, such as the Fusion, is about as concealable as a conventional belt scabbard. This offset is not without advantage. The Fusion offers a brilliantly fast draw. The angle and offset of the holster compliment a rapid draw stroke. The lock to the belt is well designed and makes for a superior paddle holster.

Of the strong-side holster types, a properly crafted pancake holster is the best choice for most of us. When properly crafted, it hugs the body and offers excellent concealment with little compromise of the draw. Good examples include the D.M. Bullard Combat and the Wright Leatherworks Predator.

INSIDE-THE-WAISTBAND HOLSTERS

For most shooters, the inside-the-waistband holster usually is the best choice. This holster rides inside the waistband, which allows the pants to conceal the body of the handgun. You don't need a long covering garment to conceal the gun; it may be concealed by a light jacket, a pulled-out sport shirt, or even a T-shirt. The IWB holster carries a compact pistol such as the Glock 19 with good concealment in all conditions. With careful study and a proper holster, a full-size pistol such as the Colt Government Model 1911 may be concealed. The SIG P220 Carry, Colt Commander, and Glock 19 are ideally suited to IWB carry, but the IWB must be properly designed. It must feature supporting leather structure that holds the holster in place with the use of belt loops or strong tool-steel belt clips. The holstering mouth must be reinforced, which allows the handgun to be easily re-holstered. A good holstering welt also keeps the handgun secure as the body moves. The Alsaker Custom Leather IWB illustrated is a good example of the proper design. Its holstering welt is present, and the Alsaker holster also features well-designed dual belt loops that offset the weight of the handgun. The Wright Leather Works holster illustrated is a highly developed design

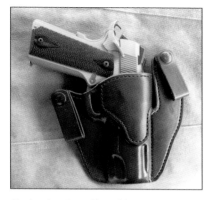

Alsaker Leather offers this custom-grade IWB. The holster's total footprint is modest, but the balance of speed and retention is excellent.

from one of our most respected companies. Note the superior blocking for fit and the inclusion of dual belt loops. These holsters will serve well for concealed carry.

Rigid Kydex offers good application in concealed carry. The draw is sharp, and the shooter finds the holster never changes shape or becomes saturated with perspiration. A problem has been that Kydex is hard and does not offer the same comfort as a leather holster. A step forward comes from Comfort Holsters. This design makes use of rigid Kydex, but also uses a gel backing for comfort. Similar to the gel-shoe inserts designed to relieve those of us who are on our feet all day, this design is effective and workmanlike.

The Wright Leatherworks IWB comes out well when molded for the snub-nosed .38. There is no faster IWB holster.

This exotic leather IWB holster from D.M. Bullard offers service-grade speed and retention. The holster will, in all likelihood, outlast the user.

The gel-backed Comfort Holster has proven a viable option in critical testing by the author.

There are a number of good inside-the-waistband holsters on the market, but each incorporates the basic criteria of a good IWB—a reinforced holstering welt and rigid belt attachment. The D.M. Bullard IWB illustrated features sharkskin covering for longevity and strong belt clips that offer a good option for rapid on-and-off fit. These clips take a good bite out of the belt. This holster is molded for my personal Colt rail gun. This isn't the easiest handgun to conceal, but the D.M. Bullard IWB does the business.

APPENDIX CARRY

If the pistol is a short-slide handgun, a conventional IWB may be used in the appendix carry. This is a holster worn in front of the body, to one side of the belt buckle. For those who have suffered a shoulder injury and have limited movement, the appendix carry is useful. For others the position is simply preferred. With a high belt line, a larger handgun may be concealed, but the short-slide handguns and the snub-nosed .38 are the natural choices for this carry. JM Custom Kydex offers a holster design with an "anti rollout feature." This holster addresses the common problem of the gun butt tilting outward when using this carry mode. The holster works as designed. Appendix carry is accessible, but the draw is seldom as fast as a strong IWB. However, with practice, some have demonstrated a sharp draw with this carry.

CROSSDRAW

Crossdraw involves the holster being carried on the weak side with the gun hand reaching over the body to draw the handgun. As discussed in the chapter on presentation, this draw is usually done incorrectly. A good crossdraw holster and the proper technique allow a good, sharp draw. The advantage of the crossdraw holster is that the handgun is accessible for the user who is seated. When driving or standing in close quarters, the crossdraw offers good access. While specialized for some of us, the crossdraw is the ideal choice for the personal lifestyle of many concealed-carry permit holders. The crossdraw design by Ted Blocker Holsters is recognized as one of the most efficient and proven types.

The holsters illustrated are among the best of the breed. There are other good makers as well. But be certain to use these guidelines as a baseline for narrowing the choice. Choose a holster with good stitching; quality material; and a balance of speed, access, and retention.

THE GUN BELT

The gun belt is a bedrock foundation of the concealed-carry rig. The holster and the spare magazine carrier must be firmly attached to a quality gun belt. A poor gun belt will stymie the ability to properly execute the presentation. The gun belt

Ted Blocker offers workmanlike designs with both open-top and thumb-break options. They have been serving the author for decades.

allows the proper implementation of techniques—the draw, presentation, and re-holstering all may be controlled, evaluated, and always executed properly. Tactics are adaptable to situations and are flexible and less predictable, but a good belt eliminates guessing.

A quality gun belt must be obtained from a holster maker. D.M. Bullard, Jason Winnie, Jeffrey Custom Leather, and Lobo Gun Leather are among those offering first-quality gun belts. You need only attempt to deploy a dress belt of the department-store variety once, and you will immediately buy a quality gun belt. Concealed-carry belts are not all utilitarian. The half-dozen I own are stylish and attractive. They are stiff without bend or flex. Some have a tactical look, but only to gun folks. Others are so polished and eye-catching they would blend in at any corporate level. Whichever holster you choose, the gun belt must be the first choice.

CHAPTER TWENTY-THREE

CARTRIDGES AND AMMUNITION

An important part of becoming a proficient shooter is obtaining sufficient, but affordable practice loads. In this chapter, we will focus on the proper ammunition to use with each caliber. Let's look at training and practice ammo first. During this discussion, I am going to provide a broad understanding of what is needed and acceptable.

Black Hills Ammunition offers many loads, among them this all-copper JHP loading.

Reliability and accuracy do not become dated. When you begin to choose the ammo, let practical application be a guide. If you enjoy hand loading, for example, a dearth of ammunition or frequent ammo shortages are less hurtful to the training budget. Everyone uses more ammunition these days, including the police, military, and handgun competitors. Consider IDPA, IPSC, police training, and even cowboy action shooting. We are using far more ammunition per shooter than ever before. This is a good thing, but sometimes the companies cannot provide all of the ammunition we need.

Those hoarding ammunition for one reason or the other have made it hard on those of us who need thousands of rounds a year for training. For practical logistics, it may be best to choose one of the more common calibers over a less popular one. I can usually find 9mm and .45-caliber ammunition at Cabela's or the local gun shop. However, there have been times when the .40-caliber stuff was scarce, and the 10mm and .357 SIG were absent from the shelves. The owner of a large shop informed me this week he has not seen .41 Magnum ammunition for a year. While I own and enjoy several firearms, many years ago I washed my hands of the oddballs. The .41 Action Express

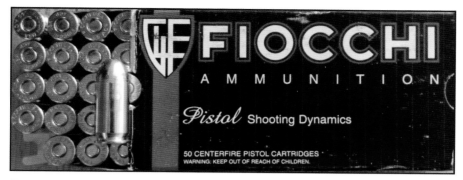

Fiocchi ammunition is an uncommon blend of good quality and affordability.

and others are interesting, and so is the .44–40 WCF, but they are not worth the time and trouble when I can get the .40 Smith & Wesson and the .45 Colt. If you enjoy one of these obscure calibers, fine, you have a capable cartridge. On the other hand, it would make little sense to choose such a caliber for the first defensive handgun.

It isn't unusual for several shooters or a gun club to pool their resources and purchase a Dillon Progressive loader. These machines are a godsend to shooters. The price isn't unmanageable for a single dedicated shooter. If you practice hard and shoot often, the machine pays for itself in a few years or less. But you have to address salient issues. Everyone isn't cut out to be a hand loader. My time and work schedule indicated some years ago that something had to give, and it wasn't going to be family time. You must be careful and pay attention to every detail. If you are a machinist, mechanic, maintenance professional, chemist, or engineer, hand loading can be easy. But when a handgun is damaged, nine times out of ten a hand load is at fault. Never buy hand loads from a buddy or at a gun show. Only reputable companies should be chosen for our needs.

PRACTICE LOADS, DIFFERENT CHOICES

Surplus Ammunition

This is ammunition declared surplus by various governments. I have enjoyed better success with rifle ammunition than pistol ammunition in this application. Some years ago, an agency purchased a supply of Egyptian 9mm. The chief did not realize the loads had corrosive primers. The SIG P226 pistols ended up rusting. The failure-to-fire rate was about 40 percent. Surplus ammunition is generally poorly suited to your needs, of uncertain origin, and should be avoided. Many years ago, the Russians ground up tons of surplus ammunition and used it for fertilizer. Seems a good plan for this ammunition to me.

Factory Remanufactured

These are loads built on the same machinery as new factory loads, but with recycled cartridge cases. I have used thousands of rounds of Black Hills "blue box" remanufactured with excellent results. Black Hills Ammunition buys tons of spent brass cases and carefully inspects them. Local shops are more likely to require a brass trade-in. This is the single most economical training resource for those who do not load their own ammunition. Either full-metal-jacket or lead-bullet loads offer viable practice at a fair price.

Factory-Generic Loads

This is the resource most of us will use when proofing handguns and beginning practice. As an example, I stock a good supply of Winchester 230-grain FMJ in the "white box" USA brand for testing .45 ACP handguns. A certain pistol may not feed every JHP bullet, and some do not like hand loads. If the pistol fails to feed, function, or fire with a quality Winchester ball, something is very wrong with the gun. It is important to proof the handgun with this type of ammunition before moving forward to training loads or personal-defense loads.

Winchester offers the USA White Box loads in the common calibers. As a rule of thumb, a fifty-round box of practice loads is priced just slightly

High Precision Downrange (HPR) offers excellent all-around service-grade loads.

more than a twenty-round box of personal-defense loads. These loads burn clean and offer good accuracy. Other resources include Fiocchi ammunition. They do not offer a specific economy line, but the ammunition is priced fairly. Federal Cartridge Company offers the American Eagle line, and Remington offers the Remington UMC loads. HPR ammunition offers a number of loads that I have found burn clean and offer good accuracy. These loads are offered in 9mm, .38 Special, .40, and .45 calibers. They are an outstanding training resource. When you begin shooting, save your brass as much as possible—you may wish to reload or purchase remanufactured ammunition later.

After you have proofed your pistol for the defense load, choose the practice load that best matches the defense load's point of impact, as regards the point of aim. Most of us will carry the 230-grain JHP in the .45, so any of the 230-grain practice loads work well. The same for 124-grain 9mm loads. Stick with this ammo, and concentrate on practicing with it, unless a real need to change surfaces.

Steel Case, Aluminum Case

Steel is cheaper and more plentiful than brass, so we will be seeing more of it from manufacturers. The foreign loads are usually OK for reliability, but powder technology overseas isn't as highly developed as American ammunition. Foreign loads are often dirty. Steel cases do not expand as readily as brass and require more force to eject.

Among a very few high-quality, steel-cased loads is the Steel Match from Hornady.

They are harder on the extractor, although I have not experienced a problem with pistol cases.

Hornady offers a steel-cased line known as the Steel Match. I have fired several hundred as of this writing with excellent results. Accuracy is what we would expect from Hornady; they are superb and function flawlessly. You do not have to pick up the cases, as they are non-reloadable.

CCI offers a line of affordable training loads as the Blazer line. Aluminum cartridge cases are light and inexpensive. (An A-10 Warthog with its 30mm gun could not get off the ground if the weapons load included brass cases, so it fires aluminum-cased ammo.) The handgun cartridges are reliable, accurate enough for practice, and offered in a wide range of loads.

A word on training loads—they are not service loads. Steel case, aluminum case, remanufactured loads, and particularly hand loads do not feature the same case mouth and primer seal used in modern service loads. Because they do not use an expanding bullet, their performance on target is limited. These are good training loads, but use only quality loads that have proven reliable in your personal handgun.

SERVICE LOADS

When choosing a service-grade load, absolute reliability and function is a million times more important than anything else. I would never chase a small gain in wound potential by using an overloaded or exotic bullet combination at the expense of reliability.

The greatest predictor of gun-

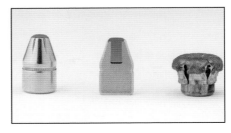

Hornady's Critical Defense loads represent the cutting edge of modern defensive-bullet technology.

fight survival remains prior training. How you perform during the battle may be unpredictable, but beyond question, you will not rise to the occasion and perform better than you have in practice. The opposite is probably true.

The single greatest factor in stopping an assailant is marksmanship and bullet placement. A 9mm JHP through the arterial region is more effective than a .45 ACP in the side. Handgun selection and caliber choice go hand in hand. As an example, few of my students are able to handle a large, double-column magazine, double-action 9mm or the 1911 .45. I can shoot the 1911 much better; I am able to deliver .45s more quickly than 9mms and to the area that will do the most good, so I have the best of both worlds.

As another example, the Glock is a great service pistol. But the .45-caliber versions stretch most hand sizes. The .40-caliber Glock 22 is a good service pistol with excellent characteristics. And despite a current fashion to rate the 9mm as effective as the .40, it just isn't so. There isn't a single 9mm loading that equals the penetration and expansion balance of the Black Hills 180-grain JHP. The Glock 22, some feel, offers the ideal compromise of hand fit, caliber, and control. Others feel that there is no compromise, and the Glock 22 is their first choice. Some 9mm load variations come close on one criterion or the other, but none equal the characteristics of the .40-caliber cartridge. So, the balance between controllability and power must be understood, and perhaps felt to understand. The Colt 1911 .45 and the Glock 22 .40 are among the best balanced and most effective of handguns per my criteria.

Big bullets produce better wound potential. This is a subject that seemed dead and put to rest more than a hundred years ago. The debate over handgun cartridges sometimes becomes ridiculous and acrimonious. The majority of the so-called research, if it was performed with any instrument other than a typewriter, is flawed. Nine out of ten people commenting on the subject have no business doing so; their qualifications don't exist. At one time, the only barometer of handgun effectiveness was word of mouth. Research into effectiveness shows that often this pipeline, coupled with verified period reports, is pretty accurate. The .45 Colt hit hard, but the .38 Colt proved worthless in military action.

Experimenters attempted to develop artificial mediums to test handgun loads. Among the earliest were pine boards. These actually proved a better comparison than most as the single most important criterion, penetration, was easily tested. Modeling clay is used to render dramatic images of bullet expansion, but this medium is completely unrealistic. Today we have repeatable and verifiable means of gauging bullet performance. The professional comparison medium is ballistic gelatin. Water testing, when done properly, is comparable. These are the only criteria worth any attention. Stories and afteraction reports are not without merit, but subject to misinterpretation and by no means a solid, verifiable resource.

While far from perfect, specially formulated gelatin has merit for comparing one load to the other. Gelatin does not necessarily represent performance in a living being, but it is used to compare one bullet or load to the other.

I have my own opinions, and while I hope my conclusions are valid, the facts are clear. We are entitled to our own opinions, but not our own facts. Studying the effect of bullets by studying the results of autopsies, and also conducting lab work, may lead to an understanding of wound ballistics. In the end, the single most important factor in stopping an attack will prove to be marksmanship. But just the same, some guns and calibers are better than

The author has the greatest respect for Black Hill's 230-grain JHP +P load. It was once called the Mack Truck of .45s.

others. Wound ballistics is a science. Conclusions drawn from studying wounds and the performance of bullets in ballistic media are valid. The results are not only repeatable but verifiable. A ballistic technician doesn't ask us to believe anything. He presents the facts, and these facts are repeatable. This is the test of science.

Stopping power studies or reports of what happens in actual gunfights are interesting, but the methods seem insubstantial to a critical observer. Assuming the validity of such a work requires a considerable leap of faith. These studies are not supported by the scientific method. In the majority of cases, the reporter cannot divulge his sources, he claims. Secret or privileged sources result in a validity of zero. The burden of proof in such reports is so weak that it would not meet the standard to be used in a small-town traffic court! They are as suspect as an anonymous complaint. The conclusions drawn are so irrelevant to the nature of personal defense that they are not worth the paper they are written on and certainly not worth your time and effort to pursue.

Military after-action reports are far more reliable. The reason our intelligence reports were so valuable during World War II is that our officers reported frankly and accurately. Many of these reports contained mentions of the effectiveness of the Colt .45 pistol. When it comes to police reports, it is a common thread that witnesses each describe an action differently. I have to be careful when I write factually, because to say I "saw the effect" means most often that I arrived just after the end of the fight. The victim might have been laid out for good, or he may have been running about, complaining of the bullet wound.

Longtime officers in high-crime areas have investigated quite a few shootings and have solid knowledge of how various handgun calibers perform. Therefore, these officers are surprised whenever someone claims the .32 Magnum or .380 ACP are enough for personal defense. Applying established, standard investigative procedures to stopping-power studies reveals bankrupt procedure.

I think citizens have a notion that police spend a lot of time on handgun and load selection. This isn't really true. Most often the agencies will choose a contract gun and its ammo for economy. Small agencies tend to offer greater latitude and some of the large agencies, particularly those with well-rounded police unions, have more choices as to caliber and handgun. The issue that is most important to these officers is usually hand fit. Police trainers do not debate stopping power. They go with what they know and concentrate on tactical movement and the application of marksmanship. If we criticize the issued weapon and ammunition—and some are far from my choice—we undermine the officer's confidence.

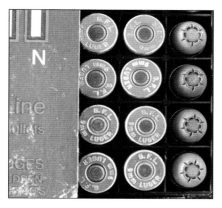

A double-action-only 9mm loaded with subsonic ammunition may not be my professional choice, but the man or woman behind the sights can make the difference. Tactics and marksmanship are important and may be more important than hotter loads in minor calibers.

For many years, professional police officers have pushed for more

Fiocchi's 92-grain Mono Block 9mm is well worth your consideration for personal defense.

Winchester's Train and Defend loads have given excellent results in the author's training classes.

training time. This reads a larger budget. Bean counters find it cheaper to bury cops than to train them. I was moved to anger in one particular incident when I read an article with some good points until the author pointed out that load selection is more important than marksmanship. He noted we could choose the load, but not where we put it! This goes against many years of police training and was a real disservice to any rookie who took that notion to heart. Shot placement in a life-or-death battle is more important than load selection. A shot with a .38 to the arterial region will work better than a .45 in the intestines. We all like to have the best load-and-handgun-cartridge combination possible, and we should choose an effective caliber and good ammunition. But the bottom line is that shot placement matters most.

All of the marksmanship rules that apply to the police also apply to civilians, something some folks do not seem to understand. You will be facing the exact same threat from the same individual as a working cop will face. Yet, you think your .380 ACP pistol will do the work of his .40-caliber pistol? Or course not! Most shootings involving civilians or cops are multiple-shot incidents and have been so since the first automatics were issued.

Two decades ago, I attended a class given by a respected medical examiner. He showed me a slide of a deceased bad guy. The fellow had a tattoo across his chest that read "Satan Lives." The bullet involved, according to the doctor, produced impressive results and actually took a chunk out of the heart. Both expansion and penetration were in the ideal range. The load, the Federal 124-grain Hydra-Shok 9mm, enjoys an excellent reputation. A few months later, I met the officer involved in the shooting. He told me the man took the shot, stopped his attack, and asked for an ambulance. The felon remained mobile until the ambulance arrived. He expired at the hospital as those with a chunk out of the heart often do. I encountered conflicting opinions of the same shooting. It appears the subject was physically able to continue the attack, but did not. Sometimes the adversary is machine-gunned in a shooting when, out of fear, we empty five .38s, six .44s, seven .45s or sixteen 9mms into the object. Those who have not been there simply do not understand the abject terror and the tyranny of the moment. If the felon is stopped, it is a stop. If not, it is a failure. It may well have been a one-shot stop we simply helped along. Dismissing multiple hits from our study eliminates most small-bore shootings. The data is flawed. If there is anything we learn

Winchester's Silvertip is a viable loading, particularly in the 155-grain .40 version.

from a stopping-power study, it's that handguns are not very powerful compared to long guns.

Once the handgun adopted is at least a 9mm or .38, tactics and marksmanship are what counts. Tactics are used to keep from being shot and to get the defensive shooter positioned for a shot. We use gelatin to model bullet effectiveness. The results of the bullet on target will depend primarily on exactly where the bullets strike the adversaries. Their levels of intoxication or addiction to drugs will also have a bearing on how quickly the bullets stop his actions.

Expanding bullets are demanded for public safety. Modern hollow-point bullets are well-designed and reliable; however, one respected medical examiner noted that about half of all hollow-point handgun bullets actually expand properly in the body. A projectile must penetrate deeply enough to create a wound that causes the loss of blood and the shutdown of a pressurized system. A big-bore bullet creates a larger wound channel. This bullet creates a larger hole and causes more blood to be let out. This results in faster shutdown of the system. There is no other way. My ideal recommendation is a loading of .40-caliber or more that penetrates a minimum of twelve inches in ballistic gelatin. The bullet should expand to 1.5-caliber diameters, but with the large-bore bullets, expansion is simply a bonus. Penetration is the single most important factor. Penetration is more than the depth of a human chest. Nor is it the widest point of the body. If the arms are outstretched in front of the threat firing at you, the bullet may need to penetrate heavy arm bones to reach the vitals. Some authorities recommend eighteen inches in ballistic gelatin. There is a factor called progression to consider. At times a bullet will tumble in the body, and the base will travel forward. This doesn't seem to happen in gelatin, but it will occur in water testing.

Progression, or tumbling, is among the reasons the original soft-lead .45 Colt loading, as one example, was so effective in creating a wound. A hollow-nose bullet that closes on a bone isn't going to expand. But experienced hunters and those investigating shootings closely feel that a bullet that strikes bone is more effective. As for the spinning, incising, and cutting of a spinning bullet, I do not give this much credence. The bullet may be moving 850 to 1300 fps, depending upon which caliber and bullet weight you use, while the cutting motion would be determined by

Impact velocity affects bullet expansion. These Barnes bullets demonstrate excellent results at different velocities.

barrel twist. A bullet may travel 18 inches in a fraction of a second in air, but not in flesh. Most .45-caliber handguns are rifled with a one turn in sixteen inches of barrel twist, but I doubt the bullet is actually turning for very long after it meets any type of material. When a bullet meets an obstacle, such as heavy wallboard, its rotation is canceled. The same would be true of bone.

Most everything I have read in the popular press, with few exceptions, doesn't agree with the reality I have studied. Some theories and so-called reports are so poorly thought out they would be laughable if the subjects were not so serious. A study that provides validity to the .32 ACP and .380 ACP cartridges by giving them an effective stop rate of over 50 percent in one-shot stops—whatever that is—has no value. The primary motivation of such a study is self-interest or self-promotion, perhaps commercial or material, not an attempt to inform and save lives. The poor scientist and preacher each tell you it is all going to be OK and evade reality.

The answer lies not simply in the caliber but in the system as well. Before you agree or disagree with me, run a difficult a combat course with your handgun of choice. Compare several handguns, including a 9mm, .40 and .45. If the big bore proves out to be a faster handgun on target and a better hitter, then couple this with superior wound ballistics, and you may have come to the same conclusion I did forty years ago. Big bullets do more damage, and accuracy can make up for power. The reverse is seldom true.

CHOOSING A DEFENSE LOAD

There are many quality makers. The individual will be able to choose a load that suits his or her needs, but service-grade reliability is the bottom line.

It may come as a surprise, but the last thing I look at in a service or defense load is the ballistic gelatin results. The first criterion must be cartridge integrity. The load must feature a good case mouth and primer case seal.

I individually soak a sample of the prospective duty load in oil, water, and solvent. After an all-night immersion, the load must fire. Those living in a true Northern climate might wish to add a spell in the freezer. Next, a single round is carefully loaded, ejected, and loaded again at least a half dozen times. (I do this safely at the range.) The bullet must have suffered no setback into the cartridge case. I test cartridge integrity in the same manner up to this point when considering revolver cartridges.

To test the revolver, I fire all the rounds but one in the cylinder, and then repeat twice. If the crimp isn't good in the loading, the bullet will jump the case forward. If the load passes these tests, and then at least fifty rounds through the handgun with perfect function, it is suitable for duty use as far as cartridge integrity goes. Next I check accuracy.

The loading must exhibit comparable accuracy to the loads I used to break the handgun in during initial practice. As an example, let's say I achieve a three-inch group at fifteen yards off of the barricade with Black Hills Ammunition 9mm remanufactured loads. I would expect the Black Hills Ammunition 124-grain JHP to perform better, perhaps a two to two-and-one-half-inch group. If this is within parameters for a service pistol, we are good to go.

A compact pistol, such as the Smith & Wesson Shield, may not be as accurate as a service pistol, but it should demonstrate the ability to group five shots into three inches at fifteen yards.

Next, I consider ballistic results. I have come to rely upon the results published by Winchester, Remington, Federal, and Speer. They are viable and reflect my own experiments. For loads without factory results available, or to check results from compact pistols, I fire into water. Water overstates penetration and understates expansion to an extent. Water results are often within 10 percent of laboratory gelatin results. I use a six-inch-wide water jug. This is simple but scientific. We may compare results of any cartridge. We may also test loads in our personal handguns. As an example, I do not expect a three-inch barrel on a 9mm to post the same velocity as a Beretta 92 with a nearly five-inch barrel. How much expansion is degraded by less velocity is what I want to see. Sometimes the load is severely handicapped, other times not. Some loads expand less and penetrate slightly more, although the velocity is less. The Speer Short Barrel line in 9mm and .45 ACP, as examples, are an answer to the question of short-barrel performance. It should also be noted that the performance I deem necessary isn't possible with a caliber below 9mm or .38 Special.

The criterion is that the loads penetrate a minimum of twelve inches of water, with fourteen inches more desirable. The bullet should achieve this penetration while expanding to 1.5 of its original diameter. This is .54 for a 9mm or .38, .60 for a .40 or 10mm, .64 for a .44 Special, and .68 for a .45-caliber bullet. It isn't difficult to find ammunition that fits these criteria.

But finding a load with a good balance of expansion and penetration in the ideal range will take some searching and effort; this load must also be reliable and reasonably accurate.

In the 9mm, there are sometimes compromises made for expansion. For example, the hottest 115-grain loads demonstrate fragmentation in gelatin and produce more than 1,300 fps from the Glock 19. They are not in the ideal range for penetration, but the reputation of the 9mm +P+ is such that allowances are made. The Cor-Bon 115-grain +P is one choice. The Black Hills 115-grain +P is another. Both companies offer 115-grain loads with modern Barnes all-copper bullets. For those preferring the Barnes bullet, these loads give good results.

Cor-Bon's highly developed loads are often found in the author's personal handguns.

I have come to prefer a heavier bullet as time goes by and I study more loads and fire them in a wide variety of handguns. Those preferring a standard-pressure load might prefer the Black Hills 124-grain JHP. However, when firing the 9mm in a full-size handgun, I find the Black Hills 124-grain JHP +P offers ideal qualities for a service load. It's not difficult to control, and the balance of expansion and penetration is good. A similar load that I have tested extensively is the Winchester 124-grain +P. The PDX Defender Winchester load is very consistent. As a further recommendation, the Winchester load offers little to no muzzle flash in dim light, an important advantage. In a load specially designed for use in a short-barrel 9mm, the Speer Gold Dot 124-grain +P is a good choice.

The .38 Special load selection is complicated, because the great majority of .38s in use for self-protection are two-inch-barreled revolvers. This means that velocity is curtailed by the lack of a full powder burn. Still, there are credible choices that offer reasonable performance. Among these is the Hornady 110-grain Critical Defense.

This load is controllable but offers good performance per my test program. Cor-Bon's 110-grain JHP has also given good results, but the +P loads should be chosen only for use in steel-frame handguns. The Speer Gold Dot 135-grain +P is specifically designed for use in snub-nosed revolvers.

The .38 revolver gets some compromise for overall performance, because the handgun isn't a service-grade sidearm; it's in the backup class.

In the .357 Magnum, there are good choices, and power isn't the concern. The goal is to find a load that is slightly below the power level offered by the Magnum and with a well-designed personal-defense bullet. A few meet these criteria.

For personal defense, the Cor-Bon 110-grain JHP is a good choice. A strong personal choice is the Winchester 125-grain PDX. The Hornady 125-grain Critical Defense has also given good results. The Black Hills Ammunition 125-grain JHP also performs well. If I were to choose a .357 Magnum service load today, it would be the heavy and hard-hitting Winchester 14-grain Silvertip.

In .40 caliber, there are many good choices. The Black Hills Ammunition 140-grain Barnes load is among the best. This load is loaded to the typical 155-grain velocity, resulting in excellent control of the 140-grain load. Expansion and penetration are good.

Moving to the actual 155-grain loads, the Hornady 155-grain XTP, the Black Hills 15-grain JHP, and the Speer Gold Dot offer credible performance. A standout, in my opinion, is the Winchester 155-grain Silvertip. It seems hotter than some loads and is at its best in a service-size pistol. Expansion is excellent.

In the big-bore revolvers, the .44 Special and .45 Colt offer a lot of good choices. In .44 Special, the Hornady Critical Defense offers ease of control and good expansion. The Speer 200-grain Gold Dot is a good all-around choice, with the availability of a Blazer practice load also using the Gold Dot bullet. Cor-Bon's DPX loading is the hottest factory load purpose designed for defense use. The effect on target is predicted to be ideal. In .45 Colt, the heavy, slow-moving bullet has proven effective since 1873. In modern loads, there are two standouts that should prove ideal for those deploying this caliber. The Winchester 225-grain PDX offers a clean powder burn and good performance. The Speer Gold Dot 250-grain JHP has also given good results.

In .45 ACP, the best choice per my research and personal testing is the 230-grain JHP. While there are differences in performance between the loads, they are more similar than different between the major players, with brand loyalty playing a role in selection.

The Black Hills Ammunition 230-grain JHP, the Winchester 230-grain PDX, and the Speer Gold Dot 230-grain are good choices. The Federal 230-grain HST has given good results. Hornady offers a +P version of the

230-grain XTP. While controllable in my Colt Rail Gun, this load isn't best suited to aluminum frame 1911s. There are a number of viable loads in 200 grains. The Hornady 200-grain XTP is respected as an accurate round, and the choice of a number of professionals. Lower recoil, greater penetration, and gilt-edged accuracy are reasons for choosing this load. The Speer 200-grain Gold Dot +P is also good.

I prefer the 230-grain weight overall, but there are lot of choices that are credible. The Black Hills Ammunition 185-grain TAC +P has delivered results that are in the ideal range for expansion and penetration. Accuracy is also good. The Cor-Bon DPX +P is another good choice that delivers excellent velocity and has proven accurate at long handgun range. For the recoil shy, the Hornady 185-grain Critical Defense load offers the lightest recoil of the popular bullet weights in .45 ACP while maintaining good performance.

The bottom line on ammunition selection for serious use is: confirm cartridge integrity first. If the ammunition doesn't feed right and does not exhibit a good primer seal and case-mouth seal, it is not service grade.

Next, the load must be accurate in your handgun. And finally, the bullet must exhibit a balance between expansion and penetration. Much of the ammunition on the market isn't service grade. Be certain the loads in your gun are.

Be certain to save your brass! Economical training hand loads are important to the high-volume shooter.

CHAPTER TWENTY-FOUR

MAINTAINING YOUR SKILL LEVEL

Practice is essential. The author finds the SIG P320 controllable.

The basic skills to handle a firearm, drive a vehicle, operate a machine, or perform complex motor skills are not innate in the human physiology. They must be learned. Once you have learned these skills, you must practice often to keep them. Handgun skills are perishable.

Successful students in my training class have acclimated to the "learning how to learn" concept by absorbing knowledge and maintaining good attitudes. They may be football players, mechanics, or musicians, but they have learned how to learn. Their attention spans are adequate, and they realize that only by application of study and repetition in the correct manner will they learn.

Others who have taken the path of least resistance in life and simply do what little they can to get by seldom profit from my training class. Perhaps they do not understand the skills needed to have a fighting chance against a motivated adversary.

The thief motivated by profit may run at the sight of a handgun. The psychopath who attacks for the pure pleasure of causing human suffering will not be dissuaded easily. Many of these felons have been shot or stabbed, and almost any that you are likely to meet have been incarcerated. Keep these likely adversaries in mind. They are not folks like us who have had a bad day. The average Joe or Jill doesn't need to be shot.

When I see people at the range, I realize most are engaging in recreational shooting, which is fine for its own sake. But these folks believe they are engaging in training for personal defense. They may think they are engaging in combat shooting, because they are firing at the B-27, but they are not. They are often shooting the X ring out of the target at seven yards. But they are not training to fight. Some stand on the static range, warm up by stretching, move their arms about in a pantomime, and then draw from an open-top holster and leisurely open fire.

Funny, they often fire the first shot slowly and then fire a flurry of shots! They are disorganized, to say the least. Some have purchased the right books. Others have not. Let the Lord watch over the ones who use television as their guide,

Some practice in traditional one-hand marksmanship will build skill.

Back to the wall, firing quickly and accurately, practice must be challenging.

because I meet them often. I have walked the streets and learned information the hard way. It is hard to pick up information any other way.

Gabriel Suarez and Tom Givens come to mind as good, modern trainers. So are the folks at Talon Training Group. Kevin Michaelowski is another whose work I respect among active writers. Massad Ayoob and I have shaken hands and see eye to eye.

All will counsel that you cannot rely on skills that you can't demonstrate.

Professional soldiers and peace officers seldom get adequate support for further training unless they are detailed to a special team. These professionals earn their keep and pay the hard way. When you are training, you must post the results and keep yourself aware of your progress. There is a need for mileposts. In personal development, I find that most of us reach a respectable degree of competency within a few months of good training, regular practice, and attention to detail. There is a steady climb to proficiency. After a year or two, you reach a certain plateau, and the increments of speed and precision come harder. That is as it should be. By the same token, these skills are perishable. If you lay off your training, you will find that your skills have eroded.

As a martial art, handgunning is probably more difficult than boxing or Karate, because much equipment is required, and you are not able to work out at home without visiting the dojo. Some of us have a long drive to the range. Dedication is required. I have

This HK VP9 has given excellent all-around results. The author continues to explore different handgun types.

The author prefers the .45-caliber self-loader overall. The One Pro is one that has given extraordinary performance.

never seen a martial artist—beginning with a young green belt I worked with—who did not excel upon application of proper principles in handgunning. Remember—learn to learn.

When you practice, the primary motivation is to maintain skill. Next, address skill-building exercises. The quantity of ammunition expended is not always the best indicator of the nature of the practice. If you enjoy shooting—and most who excel do—that's good, but do not fall into the trap of simply making brass and firing fifty or a hundred rounds at a target. The object is skill maintenance.

A professional I know well practices a drill until he cannot get it wrong. When addressing a new drill and facing a new tactical problem in competition, he solves it, and as he puts it, does not waste ammunition pursuing the drill further. Rather, he moves on to the next drill.

Too many shooters find that they are good at a certain drill and enjoy firing it again and again. Do not do so to the point that your ability to address new skills suffers. Address moving targets and skill-building exercises, such as rapid reloading, as you practice. Self-correction is difficult, but possible.

Mirror-image instruction with the instructor demonstrating the correct technique is best, but when firing alone, we may manage to address shortcomings. Confidence is built by repeating standard drills, but we must also challenge ourselves. A tight budget works against many of us. So does a crushing work schedule. I have worked eighteen months without taking off the weekend. Financially, I profited, and perhaps the public safety was served, but my body and mind were not at their best. Like many of you I have worked two and three jobs to get ahead. Something has to give, and it likely becomes firearms practice.

Controlling the Magnum isn't easy, but the author puts his time in with every dedicated carry gun.

Attention to detail, the right stance, and the proper grip must be maintained through a solid practice schedule.

Dedication and motivation must be in place. If you cannot practice monthly, then at least get to the range bimonthly. Get a good dry-fire program going.

AT HOME

You may practice dry fire at home with a triple-checked, unloaded firearm. Always dry fire against a suitable backstop that would stop the bullet. No other program is acceptable. Using the same program, the presentation may be practiced. A dozen repetitions a day is a good goal, and they should be perfect trigger breaks. After a dozen repetitions a day for a month, you will find yourself competent and in control of the trigger. The same goes for the presentation from concealed carry. You will effortlessly be presenting the handgun from concealed carry.

Here are a few drills to keep the edge.

PRACTICE DRILLS TO MAINTAIN COMPETENCE

Range Drills

For the "Bill Drill," draw and fire six rounds at seven yards as fast as you can while keeping the sight picture. All rounds should be in the X ring. Work on speed.

Draw from concealed carry and get a center hit on a target at the seven-yard line in 1.5 seconds or less. Work to achieve the same time at ten yards.

Good training is essential. These shooters are learning at Sharpshooters Range in Greenville, South Carolina.

For "Three Bull's-eyes," place three eight-inch bull's-eye targets on a target backer at seven yards. Draw and fire from left to right, re-holster, then draw and fire from right to left; put two rounds on each target. Then, draw and fire at the center target, and address either the right or the left-hand target. This drill teaches transition between targets, skill, and speed.

Practice moving with a lateral motion from one side of the target to the other side. Never cross your legs! Fire while moving. Fire with two hands at ten and fifteen yards. Fire from the barricade position at fifteen and twenty-five yards.

When possible, do the El Presidente. Shoot IDPA matches.

Home Drills

Do twelve perfect trigger compressions, at least once a week. Practice twelve rapid presentations from cover, also at least once a week.

Constant reinforcement of skills, such as firing accurately from behind cover, is demanded if you are to remain proficient.

ALSO AVAILABLE

Prepper Guns
Firearms, Ammo, Tools, and Techniques You Will Need to Survive the Coming Collapse
by Bryce Towsley

Food, water, and shelter are very important to survival. But you must also be ready to protect what is yours, because if somebody stronger, better prepared, and better equipped takes it all away, you will die. Your family will die. The only way to protect them is with firearms.

Written with the law-abiding civilian in mind, *Prepper Guns* covers the firearms and tools needed to survive, not only for defense but also for foraging. It is a comprehensive look at the realities of the firearms a prepper should have. Written by Bryce M. Towsley, a firearms expert and a full-time gun writer with thirty years of experience, *Prepper Guns* steps away from the conventional wisdom that is often spouted by prepper publishing and takes a hard, honest look at the reality of the firearms, ammo, tools, and training needed to survive at home and on the road.

If you are worried that bad things are coming and you are trying to prepare, this book is the most important piece of gear you can buy—because if you can't protect your family, your food, and your home, nothing else really matters.

$29.99 Hardcover• ISBN 978-1-63450-587-1

ALSO AVAILABLE

Shooter's Bible Guide to Home Defense
by Roger Eckstine

Learn how to safely defend your home from intruders.

When there's someone threatening at the door, will you be prepared to defend your family? If you have ever had this thought but aren't sure how to plan a proper defense of your property, this is the essential manual for you. It is your right to defend yourself and your family. However, you need to take the necessary steps to prepare for a proper defense.

Don't wait to be placed in a dangerous setting without a plan to defend your home. The *Shooter's Bible Guide to Home Defense* is an all-encompassing resource that not only offers vital information on firearms and other weapons, but also suggests the appropriate responses to many different home invasion scenarios. Examine how to:

Evaluate the premises
Choose various security systems
Safely interact with aggressors
Use body language and verbal judo
Improvise weapons

Familiarize yourself with the basics that you need to know to defend your home.

$19.95 Paperback• ISBN 978-1-62636-179-9

ALSO AVAILABLE

Gun Trader's Guide, Thirty-Eighth Edition
A Comprehensive, Fully Illustrated Guide to Modern Collectible Firearms with Current Market Values
Edited by Robert A. Sadowski

The one-stop guide to buying collectible firearms, with more than two million copies sold!

If you are seeking a comprehensive reference for collectible gun values, the *Gun Trader's Guide* is the only book you need. For more than half a century, this guide has been the standard reference for collectors, curators, dealers, shooters, and gun enthusiasts. Updated annually, it remains the definitive source for making informed decisions on used firearms purchases. Included are extensive listings for handguns, shotguns, and rifles from some of the most popular manufacturers, including Beretta, Browning, Colt, Remington, Savage, Smith & Wesson, Winchester, and many more.

This thirty-eighth edition boasts dozens of new entries since last year's edition and includes a complete index and a guide on how to properly and effectively use this book in order to find the market value for your collectible modern firearm. Determine the new prices for any firearm you want to sell or trade, whether its condition is in-box, excellent, or good. With new introductory materials that every gun collector and potential buyer should read, this book is the ultimate guide to purchasing classic or discontinued firearms. No matter what kind of modern firearm you own or collect, the *Gun Trader's Guide* should remain close at hand.

$29.99 Paperback• ISBN 978-1-5107-1092-4

ALSO AVAILABLE

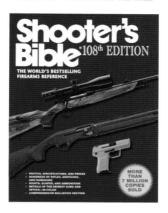

Shooter's Bible, 108th Edition
The World's Bestselling Firearms Reference
Edited by Jay Cassell

With more than seven million copies sold, this is the must-have reference book for gun collectors and firearm enthusiasts of all ages.

Published annually for more than eighty years, the *Shooter's Bible* is the most comprehensive and sought-after reference guide for new firearms and their specifications, as well as for thousands of guns that have been in production and are currently on the market. Nearly every firearms manufacturer in the world is included in this renowned compendium. The 108th edition also contains new and existing product sections on ammunition, optics, and accessories, plus updated handgun and rifle ballistic tables along with extensive charts of currently available bullets and projectiles for handloading.

With a timely feature on the newest products on the market, and complete with color and black-and-white photographs featuring various makes and models of firearms and equipment, the *Shooter's Bible* is an essential authority for any beginner or experienced hunter, firearm collector, or gun enthusiast.

$29.99 Paperback• ISBN 978-1-5107-1091-7